Jeana Marie Jeffers | 2013

Jeana Marie Jeffers

# TAGMEWRITE 101

# THE GAME
# &
# COMPLETE BOOK

AS A POETIC MUTANT
I HAVE 101 SECRET IDENTITIES
FROM THE WRITTEN CLUES
CAN YOU CORRECTLY GUESS THEM ALL
AND TAG ME PROPERLY?

# TAGMEWRITE

## CONTENTS

Dedication
Pg 3

Introduction
Pg 4

Game Rules
Pg 5

Untitled Game Poetry 1-101
Pp 6-92

101 Game Title Key
Pp 93-95

Tribute
Pp 96-97

Titled Mutant Poetry The Book 1- 101
Pp 98-185

Poetic Biography
Pg 186

DEDICATION

TO EVERYONE
AROUND THE WORLD

# TAGMEWRITE

IF YOU LOVE TO READ

THEN THIS IS THE GAME FOR

YOU

THE GAME IS CALLED

TAGMEWRITE

AND THIS IS WHAT YOU HAVE

TO DO

## TAGMEWRITE
## GAME RULES

There are 101 stories to read that differ in genre. Some are short Poems. Some are short Fictional Stories. But within every story are clues to assist YOU with identifying, WHO or WHAT, I the Author of every one of these heart rendering stories and Originator of the game is describing.

Then after YOU have evaluated the stories content, all YOU have to do next is TAG it by writing your titled guess on the line next to the stories number. The title TAGS are provided for YOU on pages 93-95.

Every story has ITS proper TAG. Therefore no TAG can be used more than once. The fact that both poetry and title are listed in numerical order does not indicate that they are the perfect match. So be careful what something might sound like, might not be right.

I included the book version of the poetry for those of you that don't like to play games. But for those of you who do, don't cheat.

### JUST HAVE FUN!

# TAGMEWRITE

**TAG ME**
**#1**_____

While skipping through this lovely garden,
I was overcome with this fixation for longevity,
For everywhere I looked was a blessed miracle,
That dripped oil across my skin with beauty.

I climbed beautiful mountains without fear,
And played with animals from every kingdom,
I took a dip in the ocean no longer polluted,
Then I stroked the flipper of the humpbacked whale.

Now tell me on what forbidden Island have I crashed,
Where everywhere I turn peace is the trumpet blast,
And where no self indulgence can rob me of prosperity?
It must be the park of imagination where real is fantasy.

*Author / Jeana Marie Jeffers*

**TAG ME**
**#2**_____

Quick!
Duck in here.
Hit the lights!
Earrrrrrrrrrrrrrongah
Earrrrrrrrrrrrrrrrrrrongah
Zooooooooooooooooooom
URRRRRRRRRRRRR
BOOM!
Maybe we would have been safer,
If you had listened to me,
And we had fled, by way of tracks.
It's your fault.
If you hadn't said hit the lights,
That would not have happened.
You didn't get hit did you?
NO!
Well let's keep it moving.
There is bound to be some more light, at the end.

*Author / Jeana Marie Jeffers*

**TAG ME**
**#3**_____

I came in a package of ten,
But oft not honor the written guarantee,
For the battle of controversy is what I maintain,
Still anything else is just a turbulence of memories.

Yet, my three branches continue to grow stronger,
Working night and day to satisfy # ones hunger,
You know the one that considers all of our needs,
Though that reality can only be realized prophetically.

So who if any truly understands my definition of justice,
When so many drastic changes keep standing between us,
All I know is that I must work harder to get it right,
And I will not stop until I hear everyone say ALRIGHT.

*Author / Jeana Marie Jeffers*

**TAG ME**
**#4**_____

Thanks Doc,
I really appreciate you seeing me on such short notice.

You are quite welcome.
Though I must first warn you,
I have never practiced psychology with anyone of your kind,
But since this month business has been a little slow,
Revamping my venue will do just fine.
So, shall we get started?
What would you like to share today?

GREAT!
So where should I begin?
Ok, Ok!
This is where it all started.
I know you heard about those ten plagues right.

# TAGMEWRITE

RIGHT!

RIGHT!

Well why did we have to come in second place?
Surely with all of us hiding in ovens and all that dough,
One of us could have raced first across that finish line.
But NOOOOOOOOOOO!
You know always a loser never a winner.

No I don't know. But!

Sorry don't interrupt,
That was just a figure of speech.
Anyway…………..
Then it was that kissing thing.
So many women were looking for their prince,
That I had to keep my lips puckered for centuries.
No decades.
Hold it which one is the longest?
Let me see a century has umm 10, 20, 40, 50, 100,
A decade has 10, 20, 40, 50, 100,
Ok for eons of years.
And do you know what everyone of them had the audacity to say,

I'm curious tell me.

Ha, Ha
I like you Doc.
Well they all said - YUK!
Every time I heard it, it just tore my poor little heart to pieces.

Well at least they didn't slap your face.

Ah!
It sounds as if you've been there before.

Back it up!
It's you on the couch not me.

Well, do you want to change?
I'm willing if you're willing.

## May 3, 2013 — Jeana Marie Jeffers

Besides, by now it is pretty obvious that I'm never going to turn into a prince.

No………..
I think I will just keep dealing with my own stack of cards.
What else you got?

How about what they did to us in Biology class and Jurassic Park.

Yes, I get the full picture now.
You must be really messed up.
So this is what I'm going to do for you.
For all your pain and suffering,
I'm going to write you a prescription for OxyContin.
Take two of those at night before you sleep,
Then you call me in the morning,
Ok.

Gee, thanks Doc.
You're the greatest.

Oh! By the way,
The whole time of my visit I want you to know that I was working on Self Control.
But I've noticed that over there in the corner you have a miniature problem with pests,
And since I don't have pockets to carry credit cards or cash,
In exchange for your services I would like to pay you for my visit - SLURP!
Sorry, I thought my offer would go over better if I just gave you a little demonstration.

Private thought.
Umm, he could be useful,
Maybe I need to reconsider the OxyContin therapy.

*Author / Jeana Marie Jeffers*

**TAG ME**
#5_____

I can be lace across your waist
A camisole where one fits ALL

# TAGMEWRITE

A charm bracelet or an anklet
A tattoo to be shared with YOU
I enjoy flirting in a field of flowers
Flying with my family of farmers
Musing far above the moth mazes
And met morphing many miracles
Think not hard for I am beautiful
The children loving me chases
The adult awes my colorful oasis
And lastly, I crawl before I walk.

*Author / Jeana Marie Jeffers*

**TAG ME**
**#6**_____

I have a humongous appetite,
That swallows everything in sight.
But only if the scales are right,
Do I sink my teeth in the over bite.

My hunger meter is a built in tremor,
That shakes me like a cold December.
After filling my belly it tries to simmer,
But the after math can be even grimmer.

So before I eat, I always sound an alarm,
Basic instinct warns there could be harm.
And that what comes next is out of the norm,
So flee everyone from the gluttonous storm.

*Author / Jeana Marie Jeffers*

**TAG ME**
**#7**_____

My relationship with you is so much like this.
I search for you and search for you,
Never, ever, does it cross my mind to give up!
Then after finding you, I love you but not right.

It is so hard to express what I feel with words.

May 3, 2013  **Jeana Marie Jeffers**

Because where you're from they're not written.
So I roll around in all your turquoise and blues.
Spending none, but good to know I'm covered.

After long days being comforted by your luxury,
I return you to the deep knowing where you are.
But don't you worry because I will not stray far.
Afraid that if I do, some pirate will take you away.

*Author / Jeana Marie Jeffers*

**TAG ME**
**#9**_____

I'm a major attraction for fascinated eyes to see.
They are mostly interested in my Sodom history.
Motivated by the tall description of me Biblically,
That is the fire to spark their let me see curiosity.

I'm a hotel chain booked with promise of resurrection.
When the time comes I just cough and VOILA, creation.
As supplier of the embalming fluid for mummification,
They experimented again VOILA, cosmetic foundation.

My number one ingredient can be hazardous to all fish.
The belief that it's impossible to drown in me is a myth.
So go with your instinct and forfeit the crazy death wish.
Thank you for your time, now listen to Beethoven's 5th.

*Author / Jeana Marie Jeffers*

**TAG ME**
**#9**_____

I've been accused of talking too much
And some things I say are untrue
And I've been guilty of slander
A breach in the partnership rule
Though I hesitate at times
Thinking before opening my mouth
But the contents within tickle my insides

# TAGMEWRITE

Until I can no longer contain the reviews

Though I am not to blame
For trifling with your great name
The blame can only fall upon your shoulders
For not being the first to keep your secrets
Especially if you don't want them to be heard
For people like me, tune in to every single word.

*Author / Jeana Marie Jeffers*

**TAG ME**
**#10**_____

I am so good to you during times of stress,
Making you forget all your troubles is what I do best.

I am not a masseur or masseuse,
But I can put your palates to good use.

When winter time comes and you need a fix,
You add me to l'eau or leche and mix.

You do me proud by placing me high on the gift list,
And if ever you stop smiling I'll blow you another kiss.

Be good to yourself but indulge carefully,
And always remember that my job is to keep you happy.

*Author / Jeana Marie Jeffers*

**TAG ME**
**#11**_____

I walk around on four legs,
But really I'm elevated.
Then when they broke one,
They said three is better.
Then they changed the design,
And I loved the transformations.
Allow me to give you a demonstration.

GREAT!
Dazzle me.

Ok over there is someone I can help.
I need to help him stack his cold medicine.
And I need to be close by his bedside.
Transform and be green to match his headboard.

NICE.
Transform again.

Ok over there is an Architect I bet he could use my help.
I need to be sturdy so that I can help him with his masterpiece.
And I need to tilt, and be equipped with a place to store his tool.
Transform and be green to match the cash inside his wallet.

AWESOME!
Do it one more time.

Ok but since this is the last one I'll make it good.
Ok see that lady over there, she looks like she needs help.
I need to help maintain her status.
So, I need to be an amazing conversation piece.
I want to be round but large enough to seat six.
I want to be completely black, to match the china cabinet.
My four legs should branch off from the balloon middle,
That supports my weight.
Transform and make the wing back chairs lime green,
So as to make all of her friends become green with envy.

Ok I see you like the color green.
But what else can you do?

I can hold books and drinks.
I can hold rooks and kings and queens.
I can hold lamps, candles, and ash trays.
I can hold pool balls and miniature tennis balls.
I can hold chips, and cards, and…..
Well if you name it, I can be it.
And the best part about it,
I just slide to second base and you place your design on first.

# TAGMEWRITE

WONDERFUL!

*Author / Jeana Marie Jeffers*

**TAG ME**
**#12**_____

While strolling through my popcorn like meadow I blow upon you my ring,
Daydreaming of the times that you need me more so than when you do not,
Calling your name requesting that you meet with me at the first sign of spring,
Though it is customary for us to wait until the harvest, therefore you cannot.
Yet, delightful is how I feel when dreaming of you consuming my peach like smile,
But nothing can compare to our copied scent of roses saturating the air,
As we roast alongside the campfire honey dipping our first born child,
Being careful not to draw undo attention, fearing others might come and stare.
So be patient my love, soon the time will come for you to enjoy the full aroma,
Therefore behold from the mountain top a beautiful orchard filled drama.
Because from there, it's impossible to miss a single pink blossom come to life,
As the stage down below appears to be covered with what looks like white ice.
So stay focused, and don't lose sight of our nature valley performance,
For we hold true to the promise of meeting all your needs, with an abundance.

*Author / Jeana Marie Jeffers*

**TAG ME**
**#13**_____

*Sing with me.*

I'm a weapon
I'm a ladder
I'm a mallet made of leather.

Woo, Too
Woo, Too
Na, Na, Na

May 3, 2013  **Jeana Marie Jeffers**

I'm a high top
I'm a stylus
I'm a rocket with a purpose.

Woo, Too
Woo, Too
Na, Na, Na

*Final Verse*
*Do Me Proud!*

I'm a stepper
I'm a cutesy
I'm a flirt within my booties.

Woo, Too
Woo, Too
Na, Na, Na

Woo, Too
Woo, Too
Na, Na, Na

*Author / Jeana Marie Jeffers*

**TAG ME**
**#14**_____

I entered the corner store totally ignoring the warnings,
For my brother had begged me to stay away from there,
Stating that the people inside were not wrapped too tight.
But this day was different for today time was on my side,
I had 20 minutes to kill until the bus to work would arrive.
So, because I was craving for an ice cold bottle of coca cola,
And that was the only available place to satisfy my desire,
I thought that if I'd be quick about it, I might not get caught,
Especially since no other patrons were inside to finger me.
So I did what I knew to be the correct thing to do,
And that was to approach the man behind the counter,
Doing so with a mild spirit because my day was going right,

# TAGMEWRITE

I then said. Good morning Sirs, acknowledging security also.
I would like to purchase please a nice cold bottle of Cola.
Then right at that very moment three other ladies entered.
Each of them walked right up to the counter and lined up,
I greeted them all, but none accepted the deliverance.
Then the man behind the counter colored me invisible.
He said to the first woman, how can I be of assistance?
She requested a pack of cigarettes and some chewing gum,
He rung her up, she surrendered her cash, thanked him,
He reciprocated and added look forward to seeing you again.
Then she left and he replayed the scenario of ignorance over.

To the second woman he said, how can I be of assistance?
That is when I said, while trying to remain calm.
Excuse me Sir but I was here first.
Can I please get that cold bottle of Cola? I have a bus to catch.
He said. In a minute! The longer it sits the colder it gets.
The security person snickered from behind his newspaper,
And the second woman rolled her eyes at me as if I was wrong.
Then she said to the man behind the counter,
I need some aspirin for my splitting headache,
And could I please get some liniment for the pain in my joints?
The man behind the counter said. Right away you poor thing.
Then he looked at me as if to say, now don't you feel ashamed.
It might sound crazy but I did, feel a little ashamed,
Yet flying above that were the feelings of regret,
For I have not seen the cross over from this stationary time zone.
So I waited, though now with a limited amount of patience.
For my 20 minutes was fast depleting,
And my assurance to be on time for work was quickly fleeting.
But like a nincompoop I allowed my addiction to ground me.
And once more the man behind the counter said,
To number three, with a certainty was not me.
How can I be of assistance?

Now you would have thought but maybe not,
With her witnessing a for sure case of disrespect more than twice,
That she would have done everything within her power to be nice,
But in the case of inferiority, it plays second fiddle to superiority.
Therefore lady three request from the man behind the counter,
Assistance with an item on the same side of the room as she,
Some bottled incense, because she could not decide on a fragrance.

Of course that was right up his alley.
So it became very obvious, that none of them cared about my needs.
And when that door opened once more,
And two others entered,
I recalled what my brother had said about their interior wrappings.
I knew then it was time to go,
For the urgings of Cola was making me old grow.
So I snatched my two dollars that I had laid on his counter,
Then I ran out the door with a great deal of frustration for the bus.
But as I was running to the next block towards the bus stop,
I heard this voice yelling stop thief.
When I turned to look it was the security officer from the corner store.
Well I had no business with that man,
Surely he could not be yelling at me.
So I continued running,
But for some strange reason I started to get extremely tired,
My legs felt weak and my heart felt like it was about to stop.
I'm a young person could I be experiencing withdrawal from the lack of Coke?
No that's crazy, that can't be the reason.
Well whatever was going on with this body,
It was slowing me down and no way would I make it to work in this condition,
So I ducked into a nearby alley and decided to address the situation.
But those weak knees of mines gave out and I fell, landing flat on face.
I managed to drag my body behind a trash dumpster,
Then I covered up with this white sheet that someone had tossed away.
I figured that along with the trash dumpster would hide me from security,
Just in case it was me that he was pursuing,
Even though I know I did nothing wrong.

I must have blacked out,
Because when I took a peek from under that white sheet,
The dumpster had been moved and I never heard them move it.
And I was now lying on my left side facing two strangers who looked like paramedics.
I recognized their uniforms because the guys that came to take my brother away,
They were wearing the same identical blue and white attire.
I asked them how they knew where to find me?

# TAGMEWRITE

The one kneeling beside me said. We received a 911 call that someone was in distress.
The caller was a Female, who chose to remain anonymous,
But she gave us a complete description and location.
He then said. Now I want you to lie completely still because your situation is critical,
And we are afraid that if we move you that it could kill you.
I said. Kill me what in the world is going on? I promise to never drink another coke.
He smiled and looked beyond me.
I said who are you looking at?
Is that security guy behind me?
He said. Yes but how did you know?
I said because I can feel him.
That is when I requested that they completely remove from my body the white sheet,
Then tried to roll over to take a good look at the man behind the newspaper,
But the security man was preventing me from rolling on my backside,
He was applying steady pressure to the center of my back.

I demanded an explanation as to why he was touching me.
He said. For the past 15 minutes I've been trying to stop the bleeding.
I said. Stop the bleeding, why am I bleeding?
He said. Because you have a bullet lodged in your back.
Then it got real crazy.
I said. Who shot me?
Then there was total silence.
Security then said it was me.
I yelled for you to stop but you kept right on running.
I said. So you were yelling at me, but why I hadn't done anything wrong?
He said because it's my job to stop a thief.
And right then I lost it.
Thief! Thief!
Why I've never stole anything in my entire life.
He said I'm not going waste my breathe arguing that point with you little lady,
So as it has already been stated,
You need to calm down and lie still.
All this excitement is only aggravating your condition.
And what I'm trying to do right now is offer you a helping hand.
Then I said. So now you want to help me.
What's the problem your conscience bothering you?
The security guy replied. No my conscience is fine.

May 3, 2013    **Jeana Marie Jeffers**

Bottom line,
If it comes down to choosing between YOU,
And keeping a roof over the head of my family,
Well if business is slow, then I call out a thief.
But if you persistently say that there is no thief,
Then that puts my job on the line,
Therefore one of us has got to go.
And it surely is not going to be me.

Internal thought.
You have got to be kidding.  I must be having a nightmare.
I then responded.  But you shot me in the back,
And you don't find anything wrong with that?
Security Man then states.  No I was aiming for your leg,
But then you tripped and stumbled.
And that's the story that I explained to the officer over there,
Along with these two paramedics here trying help save your life.
Save my life.  You missed that opportunity back at the corner store,
When you sat by and did nothing,
From the moment I walked through the door.
No! You thought that Owners disrespectful behavior was funny,
And just sat there reading that stupid newspaper as if all was good.
And then like a fool you accuse me of stealing,
Chase after me for nothing and then shoot me.
Take your hands off me I'm probably better off dead.
The only mistake I made was not listening to my brothers warning,
And for that I will never be able to enjoy the taste of Cola again.
What I don't understand is the fact that you are a black man,
How can you stand by and not get involved for a righteous cause?
He said I did when I came after you for stealing that money on the counter.
And I did the exact same thing two months ago on the night your brother died.
And his last dying words were the same as yours,
I didn't do it!

*Author / Jeana Marie Jeffers*

**TAG ME**
**#15**_____

They said it was I, who played a role in the first sin,

# TAGMEWRITE

But they don't know they weren't even there.

I don't like speculation it's bad for my reputation,
And to accuse me without evidence is very unfair.

The second lie told, was that I practiced medicine,
And that lie turned Jekyll into Hyde and me into sauce.

So, I demanded after witnessing their perjury for a retrial,
For it is not I who lied, what they are spreading is false.

But the judge said SILENCE! Order in the court!
Then said, Are you, or are you not, the pupil of the eye?

*Author / Jeana Marie Jeffers*

**TAG ME**
**#16**_____

I want to shower your hair in the sweet scent of Apricot.
I want to feel at home with you,
So you can shine like Crimson in the window.
I want to petal my Lavender straight to your soft bath water.
I want to lay bare on your white Linen and watch you fall asleep.
I want to dip you like Orange sherbet as we dance the night away.
I want to taste your Peach body sugar,
As I run my tongue across your shoulders.
I want to kiss your shaded Pink lips until the moon is no more.
I want to place upon your Russet finger,
That love knot that will forever tie us together.
I want to seal our bloodline with Scarlet,
Because I screened our DNA and we're compatible.
I wanted to be sure to include Yellow,
Because I knew this one was your favorite.

These are the romantic words that the real Man in your life will utter,
Right after he personally hands you one by one, all ten forgive me's.
Then of course you say, but not in that exact order right. (SMILE)

*Author / Jeana Marie Jeffers*

May 3, 2013 — Jeana Marie Jeffers

**TAG ME**
**#17**_____

I represent the conscience of families everywhere.
And my creator made me animated with big blue hair.
Of which I choose to say is a representation of the sea,
But like it you really don't want to ever aggravate me.

My green dress was designed to cover the world over.
We therefore root our trees for generations to handover.
Though I do not understand the beads and shoes of red,
But I'm guessing they symbolize the ground is being feed.

Oh how I do try very hard to keep my family in line.
Let me see you keep it together with miracle like minds.
It can only be a dream to wish for one big happy family.
But just do your best and remember to turn OFF that TV.

*Author / Jeana Marie Jeffers*

**TAG ME**
**#18**_____

Scoot over!
You're invading my space.

Well excuse me your highness,
This load has me feeling a little bloated,
And that is why I rocked in your space.
I was only trying to balance.

Bloated, Balance,
Those are two words I never want to hear.
They could only mean one thing,
That I'm going to work that much harder,
To sweat out all that excess water.

That's right!
Just ignore the fact that I'm over worked too.
I'm getting a little tired of all our conversations,
Spinning off in one direction,

And then they recycle and end up being about you.

That is just not true.
I care ….
Hey!
You know what!
Something crazy just popped up.
Instead of us working side by side,
They should have put me on top.

Why?
Do you think that all of your complaining
Would go over better if you were on top of me?
Well think again partner!
I don't want all your nasty sweat rolling down my back.

No.
I was actually thinking along the lines of my weight
Helping you stay in your place.

Man.
You had better shut your trap immediately,
Or you're going to regret it when I throw something
Dirty up in it.

What did I do now?
That is just like a woman,
Always taking what you say out of context.

*Author / Jeana Marie Jeffers*

## TAG ME
#19_____

I'm stronger than steel,
Your bare frame sex appeal,
My diploma supports the Anatomy field.
Was used as a prank in the house of thrills,
Surgically removed so she could come alive,
After touching those of Elisha he was revived,
Without me YOU would certainly be deprived.
So get milk, then I can bust a move and survive.

## May 3, 2013 — Jeana Marie Jeffers

Whew! It's hard being me.
Ha, Ha, Ho, Ho, I made a funny.

*Author / Jeana Marie Jeffers*

**TAG ME**
**#20**_____

Your collapsible source of shade will be incomplete,
 As they search for my cure throughout many holes.

But, I'm complicated and conceal myself amid the fog.
Traveling great distances and breaking international laws.

Then after my precipitating values have both intermingled,
They settle like dewdrops giving birth to aquatic disasters.

In the past, my treatment was an enormous sliver of lime.
But, for future reference,
Quit smoking the pipes and everything will work out just fine.

*Author / Jeana Marie Jeffers*

**TAG ME**
 **#21**_____

The human tongue can be hypocritical,
And if used improperly can send a mixed signal.
Though my tongue as well is two directional,
I do not ignore my tongues guiding principles.

For if I do,
Ignore the prodding's of my fork in the road,
Then when I'm hidden in the bush,
With my radar aimed at you,
And unzipping skin to lighten my load,
Instead of exercising the right,
I would renounce my will to crush,
Instead of loving the hunt,
I would hate the pursuit of warm blooded stew,
All of which would go contrary to nature,

# TAGMEWRITE

Therefore I would be just as swishy washy as YOU.

*Author / Jeana Marie Jeffers*

**TAG ME**
**#22**_____

I tried touching my face in the watered reflection but I disappeared.
It must have been a contrast of heaven that made me look in there.

Wilting from the swallowed sand my perspiration caused to evolve.
I see rising above the sun, giant bees, palm trees and even Taj Mahal.

I finally reach a nice cool place to spread the news of feathered glory.
But same as Gideon's Angel had vanished so did the end of this story.

*Author / Jeana Marie Jeffers*

**TAG ME**
**#23**_____

Oh Kachoo you are such a romantic,
Breathing all down my neck,
That fresh scent of sunflower fragrance,
I know you've come to make your proposal,
But I would like to get better acquainted,
Then maybe I will accept your seeded gifts.
And even though you're looking mighty fly,
In that red-breasted suit,
I'm a lady and desire to be courted properly,
Though I'm thankful that your gift wasn't slimy,
Seeing me gag on a rope is not very lady-like,
Ok! Go ahead and do your thing.  Woo Me.

*Author / Jeana Marie Jeffers*

**TAG ME**
**#24**_____

Wow where do I begin.
You know that you asked me a two part question.
How did I get started in this business?

**May 3, 2013** — Jeana Marie Jeffers

So I'm going to start by separating the two.
I am not a business or industry,
Those are labels that the money makers invented.
And they came on the scene way, way after me.
In fact, my existence started with the very first syllables.
He spoke something meaningful,
And wrote them down on a note pad,
Then magically what he spoke came to life.
And there I was dancing across the broadways.

You see,
I also work in conjunction with a mood.
It can be a good mood or a bad mood.
A happy mood or a sad mood,
Insane or sane,
Affectionate or moody,
I don't question it.
I just perform it.
I give it harmony,
Connect the thoughts with the results,
And then I am placed on a rhythmic scale.
Though your imagination is what sets the tone.

That's beautiful.
Thank You

*Author / Jeana Marie Jeffers*

**TAG ME**
**#25**_____

I was formed out of clay,
And was shaped into a legend,
And though I did not eat much humble pie,
My strong convictions turned out pleasant.

I've been idolized and VILIFIED,
During the course of my glorious years,
But I stayed ready, and kept to the count,
And spoke poetic trash in defense of my career.

# TAGMEWRITE

I am the Greatest.
You are the Greatest.
Yes he is the Greatest.
And now it is unanimous.

*Author / Jeana Marie Jeffers*

**TAG ME**
**#26**_____

Sharper than a two edge sword,
Lamp to your foot,
Light to your roadway,
Cannot speak a lie,
Survived the test of time,
And have made the bestsellers list.

**TAG ME**
**#27**_____

Day One
Crack
Oh LORD I can hardly move.

Day Two
Crack
Oh LORD this day is worse than the first.

Day Three
Crack
Oh LORD can you help me I'm stuck.

Day Four
Crack
Oh LORD
Thank you!
For today I only feel it in my knees.

Day Five
Crack
Oh LORD my fingers are stiff,
Can you strengthen me so I can open this jelly jar?

May 3, 2013   **Jeana Marie Jeffers**

Day Six
Crack
Oh LORD
Thank You!
For it is a beautiful day

Day Seven
Crack
Oh LORD
Thank You!
I am not going to complain,
For tomorrow I have to start the process all over again.

*Author / Jeana Marie Jeffers*

**TAG ME**
**#28**_____

Ok do I want to go to the store?
Or should I sit here and watch TV?
Did I put those shoes over there?
Where in the world is Marvin?

Wait a minute.
Wasn't it Marvin who told me to stay black?
No what he had said was,
Never mind who cares about what he said.

I'm not sure which side of the track I belong.
And what does that mean anyway?
I've seen a whole bunch of people switching sides.
Either you do or you don't which one is it?

Make up your mind you are taking too long.
That's what Marvin said I'm dead in the head.
Was he serious or was he making a joke?
Oh well I guess I'll go to the store.

*Author / Jeana Marie Jeffers*

# TAGMEWRITE

**TAG ME**
**#29**_____

My goodness it's freezing cold in here.
No I think you're mistaken it's burning up.
No you're wrong it's shivering cold.
No you're wrong I'm sweating bullets
Ok who turned up the heat?
No! Who turned it down?
Oh shut up!
Why don't you both take a chill pill!

*Author / Jeana Marie Jeffers*

**TAG ME**
**#30**_____

I think you're fat,
I think that you're ugly,
I hate your guts
Without any rhyme or reason,
Your existence makes no sense,
So my goal is to end all the suspense.
But, there is one thing I like about you innocent FOES,
You make it easy to plant inside your minds my WOES.

*Author / Jeana Marie Jeffers*

**TAG ME**
**#31**_____

Thump, Thump
Thumpa Thump.
Thump Thump Thump Thump
Thumpa Thump.
Thump, Thump
Thumpa Thump.
Thump Thump Thump Thump
Thumpa Thump.
HEY!

That's the music I bring to the BYOF party.

May 3, 2013  **Jeana Marie Jeffers**

But I wonder why the hostess changed the party status to BYOF?
I guess some invited guess has a serious problem with self control.
Well no problem, I think I have enough on this platter to go around.

Chomp.
Ooh that taste good.
Chomp.
Umm I like that too.
Let me try something on the other side of the tray.
Chomp.
Ooh Yummy!
Chomp, Chomp, Chomp, Chomp.
Oh shucks!
It's all gone.
Now what am I gonna do?
Maybe someone else brought plenty,
And they won't even notice that I didn't bring any.
Besides they all jump when they hear my music,
So I think everythang is gonna be alright.

Thump, Thump
Thumpa Thump.
Thump Thump Thump Thump
Thumpa Thump.
Thump, Thump
Thumpa Thump.
Thump Thump Thump Thump
Thumpa Thump.
Hey!

Oh Lord there he is and look, once again he showed up empty handed.
What we gon do Lizzie?
Hide!

*Author / Jeana Marie Jeffers*

**TAG ME**
**#32**_____

They call me cabbage patch kid, but I look more like Bok Choy.
They call me snow, but I'm a tasty green legume.

# TAGMEWRITE

I like to soak my feet in water, but I'm not a nut.
According to the character writing about me I'm one of the best tasting beans.
And I'm a magnificent spice that can also be taken as a medicine
Our other cuisinart relatives are Uncle Stir Fry, Papa Pan Fry, and Good ole Grand-Daddy Deep Fry. And don't forget about Aunt Sushi, Momma Wonton and Grand-Ma Rangoon.

*Author / Jeana Marie Jeffers*

**TAG ME**
**#33**_____

I protect you from those rainy days,
And put back for vacations on the way.
There are times when predators clock me,
But those violators provide no necessity,
For my institution is built on trust,
And will charge the fee of handcuffs.
Though some might escape to a Netherland,
Stealing from me is no mere walk in the sand,
Because I have a close friend living by the shore,
And wouldn't you know it,
She bears the same name as me,
And with interest will collect ALL lost currency.

*Author / Jeana Marie Jeffers*

**TAG ME**
**#34**_____

It's not much of a parade, when I see you slip and slide.
When they say stay off the streets, you should abide.

The ocean is fierce, especially during this time of year.
So anticipate the thunder, and some major tail spins.

That ice cream cone that you eat from the front yard,
It's a hurricane special, swirling to whip frozen custard.

Though the marvel footage seems to be shot on camera,
I say don't chase the funnel or you might get hammered.

*Author / Jeana Marie Jeffers*

**TAG ME**
**#35**_____

Let me wipe the smudges from my eye.
So I can be your Hubble of the dark sky.
I can see above the deep magnetic hole.
Amazed at how math plays a visible role.

When I lie down, I race back to the top.
And aim my Monocle on the Astronaut.
Walking in boots would be astronomical.
But I'll settle for viewing the phenomenal.

*Author / Jeana Marie Jeffers*

**TAG ME**
**#36**_____

I'm flying through the air with the greatest of ease,
Departing my verbs, de, de, de, de,
Ooh Weeeee!
Hick Up!
I'm hanging in the air, rah, rah, rah, umm care.
No!
Suspended in the air, oh look, Niagara Falls.
Hick Up!
Ok, that's enough my speech is slurred,
No, Subject Impeded.
Time to get to the other side of this,
Rah, rah, rah, umm trapeze.
Dang!
What's that net?
Ah beautiful rope.

*Author / Jeana Marie Jeffers*

# TAGMEWRITE

**TAG ME**
**#37**_____

I make it all about YOU.
That is what Momma said to do.
She did not say it because she was humble.
But because she did not want to see ANYONE stumble.

Momma said to smile is a blessing from above.
So that is my gift to YOU and I give it with love.
If WE do our best to follow the fine example set by Mother.
Then WE can willingly accept that WE are BLOOD Brothers.

So now I'm going to introduce to YOU,
The woman responsible for my existence,
I now humbly, lovingly, and willingly give YOU my Mom.
THE GOLDEN RULE!

*Author / Jeana Marie Jeffers*

**TAG ME**
**#38**_____

My chemical components are plant ashes and seaweed.
I don't swim with the mermaids but lavish with Jacuzzis.
I'm a variety basket of perfumed scents and colorful dyes.
Make you feel like silk while sipping on a glass of Sunrise.

*Author / Jeana Marie Jeffers*

**TAG ME**
**#39**_____

Doppler - I try hard to keep things civilized around here.
But you bronco's just insist on being divided.
You run in packs,
Trying to see which one of you can outrun the other.
You fight one another and you're of the same color.
And they say we're wild, and hard to tame.

Now let's go over this one more time.
Repeat after Me!

### Jeana Marie Jeffers
May 3, 2013

I Dark Moon, Little Moon, Silver Moon, Grey Moon,
Brown Derby Splash and Herbie,
Dark Moon - Herbie! Naw not Herbie.
Yes Herbie.
Dark Moon - But he's just an Ass.
Herbie - Excuse Me!
I'm part Ass and part Horse that makes me a Mule.
Get a clue!
Doppler - You see, Herbie is part of the Herd family.
So are you going to say it or not?
(RELUCTANT)
Ok.
I Dark Moon, Little Moon, Silver Moon, Grey Moon,
Brown Derby, Splash and I Herbie,
Promise to do better and be more like Doppler.
(GRUMBLING)
Promise to do better and be more like Doppler.
Because if we don't.
Because if we don't.
All the other paints are going to be done away with.
And there won't be anything left but black and white.
All the other paints are going to be done away with.
And there won't be anything left but black and white.
Thank You!
Now go somewhere and do some grazing.

(TROTTING AWAY WITH HERBIE BRINGING UP THE REAR)
Splash - Ok, although I'm safe.
Refresh my memory.
How did Doppler become leader of the pack?

Grey Moon - He's the fastest runner out of the pack.
He must have got in lots of exercise in his country.
And he studied magic there.
He said that is how he earned his stripes.
So do you want all of us to end up looking like him?

Splash - NO! I like my paint.

Doppler - Then be very, very careful not to start a stampede,
Or try to buck the order of things.

# TAGMEWRITE

Splash – Where did he come from?
Herbie – He's also very sneaky.
Dark Moon – Well he can stay up front.
You can't miss him, he's a bull's-eye.
(EVERYONE LAUGHING)

*Author / Jeana Marie Jeffers*

**TAG ME**
**#40**_____

Well my story is probably not as touching as hers.
But I would follow her for life wherever she goes.

Though we do have something we share in common.
Her brother and my sister, share the same time space.

Though this is how we differ, sister did not get first choice.
I trusted our maker knew who would be the perfect match.

And that He did, He placed us exactly where we belong.
So I feared for nothing, forgetting that this is His song.

I'm truly happy that it was Day and I to be united.
Sister winks every new horizon and says to us, Great Job!

Oh how I do love it, when my energy lights up Days smile.
And watching her skip through the seasons set to my dial.

But this is not about a love story between me and the Day.
It is about making sure that each of us rises their own way.

*Author / Jeana Marie Jeffers*

**TAG ME**
**#41**_____

Let me blow on your hair like King Kong.
Caress your face until the height of dawn.
Our love comes at you from all directions.
A truce is called for the day of inspection.

May 3, 2013  **Jeana Marie Jeffers**

Not everything we toss at you is vanity.
Instability enables us to keep our sanity.
Although we want very much to commit,
But we would be tempestuous hypocrites.

And if not for the four Angels persistence,
This breezy affair would fly in the distance.
So we're working on staying nice and calm.
And respect the wishes of God's Kingdom.

*Author / Jeana Marie Jeffers*

**TAG ME**
**#42**_____

I don't want to hear it.
I don't want to hear it.
You know they say that music can soothe the soul.
I don't care!
I don't want to hear it.

I don't want to see it.
I don't want to see it.
You know they say that beauty is in the eyes of the beholder.
I don't care!
I don't want to see it.

I don't want to feel it.
I don't want to feel it.
You know they say love is what makes the world go round.
I don't care!
I don't want to feel it.

I don't want to taste it.
I don't want to taste it.
You know it has been said,
Taste and see that the LORD is good.
I don't care!
I don't want to taste it.

# TAGMEWRITE

I'm not going to do it.
I'm not going to do it.
You know it has been said,
That there is more happiness in giving than there is in receiving.
I don't care!
I'm not going to do it.

Your reluctance to take advantage of using your good senses,
That says much about the kind of person you are.

So, just who do you think I am?

I'm not going to tell you.
I'm not going to tell you.

*Author / Jeana Marie Jeffers*

**TAG ME**
**#43**_____

I wonder what it would be like,
If I just up and ejected everyone in outer space?

There would be no more Crime or Injustice.
There would be no scent of Hatred in the air.
There would be no more Starvation or Malnutrition.
There would be no Verbal, Physical or Mental Abuse.
There would be no more Stealing or acts of Violence.
There would be no more Pollution spread everywhere.
There would be no more War of any sort soiling the core.
There would be no more Lies told in white or living color.
There would be no more Forest Fires destroying my seeds.
There would be no more causes of Death used to fertilize my hair.

But wait!
Unless that is the perfect plan, I just can't eject,
All that bad stuff up there in outer space,
For that would not be justifiable or even done in good taste.

No, I need to keep them right here where they belong,
Detained and in my custody,
Then ground them for committing all those major atrocities.

Yes, that is exactly what I'm going to do.
 I'm just going to continue right on hanging in there,
And wait on our loving Creator to make me brand spanking new.

*Author / Jeana Marie Jeffers*

## TAG ME
#44_____

At the peak of dawn I can still see you,
Winking at the Owl going Who, Who,
All the while the time table is spinning,
In comes the cycle with a new beginning.

I beckon for your attention when half full,
Though justice is eclipsed by divine rule,
Laughing at the sparks tickling my insides,
Joyful as we pass to give another high five.

I bring out the best in lovers everywhere,
Listening to Michael sing Got to Be There,
Yet some do whisper look up at the lunatic,
They still love seeing this faithful night flick.

*Author / Jeana Marie Jeffers*

## TAG ME
#45_____

Oh Boy!
Yawning
Here I go
Time to take my winter nap
And during the course of my slumber
I will dream about what we share in common
The dipping of our fingers in the honey jar
What a tasty thrill!
But first I need a piece of bark
To floss that Salmon stuck between my teeth
Let me see

# TAGMEWRITE

What's next?
Oh yeah!
Time to take a quick shower
In the waterfall right outside my den
That way I'll be nice and clean
So here I go
Entering my nice and peaceful retreat
Placing behind me that nagging female
So here I go
Time to get some sleep
Yawn and Stretch
Goodnight!

*Author / Jeana Marie Jeffers*

**TAG ME**
**#46**_____

I'm there for you when things get at their worse.
I'm even there whenever you need to converse.
When I broke down and had fallen by the wayside,
Both you and I sat together and shared our cries.
And as we look at one another's imperfections,
All we recognize is the same identical reflections.
And we're willing to make the ultimate sacrifice,
So let us etch ourselves a legacy in history for life.

*Author / Jeana Marie Jeffers*

**TAG ME**
**#47**_____

Surrounding you with loveliness is my way of protecting you,
Like the thorns blossoming above our heavenly bridegroom.
Though in this honorable system I do wear the golden trophy,
As I lavish gray-headedness with a spruce of fame and glory.

The women in your life bring praise to their beloved families,
Their heads showered with the gems from Jacob's fountain.
If they wear me proud the title will be earned your majesty,
And no one will be able to lift the headdress of your authority.

As for the little ones they want to be footstep followers,
As they mimic me with braided hair and honorable flowers.
Yet with me they will continue to achieve their royal dignity,
As they rise with scepters in hand above educated poverty.

*Author / Jeana Marie Jeffers*

## TAG ME
#48_____

I feel congested because you left me broken.
So I sought out Humpty Dumpty,
To ask how he put the pieces back together.
He said.
First they tried to use reverse psychology.
Yelling Humpty,
Why don't you try and pull yourself together.
But that didn't work.
He said.
For my chambers were in total disarray.
Then they tried using some super glue.
But the shape came out totally wrong.
One side was up and the other was down.
So then finally, they took me to see a surgeon.
And what he did I will never forget.
I then said, with a tiny bit of excitement.
Something I haven't felt in a very long time.
Tell me Humpty what did he do, for you?
He said and I mean the surgeon.
Humpy, I have some good news and some bad,
How do you want it?
Humpty said.
Let's start with the bad.
Well this one is so badly damaged,
And there is no possible way to repair it.
But here's the good news.
I'm just going to give you a new one.
Humpty said.
YEAH!
I said.
WOW!

# TAGMEWRITE

That day I learned two things.
 I was replaceable.
And Humpty was like Frankenstein.
He let the weight of this world make him crack.
To the point of where he needed a new brain.
So I left there with a whole new outlook on life.
Rejecting all that cholesterol bull you feed me.
And unlike Humpty,
 I will always maintain my unique composition.
Because like lovely Aaliyah said,
 I CARE FOR YOU.

*Author / Jeana Marie Jeffers*

**TAG ME**
**#49**_____

I'm a preservative as seasoning is to food.
Sliding down soft mountains till the river is full.

I hide within the cliffs of an emotional estate.
Then the wind triggers a smear of bitter taste.

I rinse I wash, the island filled with debris.
Dropping crystals in the sockets like detergent.

But when it rains it pours, the words of fame.
Blink and the crocodile will clog up your drain.

*Author / Jeana Marie Jeffers*

**TAG ME**
**#50**_____

I'm a Hybrid.
I'm fifty percent heavy metal.
My better half she's modifiable.
How today's women are made.
Give them five stars for GREAT.

*Author / Jeana Marie Jeffers*

May 3, 2013 — Jeana Marie Jeffers

**TAG ME**
**#51**_____

I want it.
I love it.
Will one day have it!
I need it.
So I grab it.
And now it's all mines.
I'm the proud owner of,
This seize the moment TAG.

*Author / Jeana Marie Jeffers*

**TAG ME**
**#52**_____

I hang out on the corner with my man fearless fly.
But if we don't change our habits he or I could die.
Though he's know to get around faster than me,
One quick tug on my rope, I propel as if I had wings.

I love adventure, so I spy on humans when they read.
Sugar head fearless gets caught, so I go set him free.
I'm not a super hero, but oh how I do love the hype.
But it's time for me to bounce, or my y-fee, will bite.

*Author / Jeana Marie Jeffers*

**TAG ME**
**#53**_____

Slipping in and out of life with nowhere to go and nowhere to be,
I decide to take a few trips and see what challenges awaits me.
So the first place I listed was a visit to Egypt.

So there I was surrounded by kilns of limestone,
Ready to assist my Brothers and Sisters erect the Great Sphinx.
After about one week of hard labor I decided my work was done.

# TAGMEWRITE

It was now time for me to move on.
But making my departure wasn't easy.
Those Egyptians weren't too fond of the word freedom.
In fact they were advocates of slave labor.
So like Moses I high tailed it up out of there.
But I did not have to part the red sea.
I allowed modern technology to set me free.

The second place on my list to visit was Rome.
I must have had my timing off,
Because I was going there to help erect the Coliseum,
But I ended up in the arena as a Gladiator ready for combat.
So quickly I pushed the button on my metal vest.
But if I had been one second off then it would have been curtains.

I then set my sights on China.
Great just in time they have probably a mile or two left to go.
So the next eight hours we work shoulder to shoulder.
Then we look back and say, mission accomplished. 任务完成
They said it in their language and I just nodded.
Then they said, 吃的时候
I wasn't sure what that meant
But after being lead to the dinner table,
I knew they must have said.
Time to eat!
But after taking one look at the spread,
It did not look anything like what they serve in the U.S
So as not be disrespectful or insulting,
I pushed the button.

There are many more places that I would like to visit and lend a hand.
But right now I really would like to just go forward.
And since I have no idea what the future holds.
I'm just going to return me and my wonderful invention to the present.

*Author / Jeana Marie Jeffers*

**TAG ME**
**#54**_____

Hint,

May 3, 2013     **Jeana Marie Jeffers**

With me you can be anything that your heart desires,
You can be a superhero that comes to save the day,
Where everyone is puffing up your chest with Hooray!

Hint, Hint
But there are many times when I extinguish your fire,
I simply flip the script deflating your chest undercover,
Then you toss, turn, and sweat until you foolishly blubber.

Hint, Hint, Hint
Most of me you forget, but others you dig deeper to hire,
Someone more lucid than thou to X-plicate my true definition,
But to justify their cause, they label me as mere premonition.

Hint, Hint, Hint, Hint and that be four
I'm a speedy Z-mystery for all my fallen subjects to inquire,
Though I'm not to be confused with the story of Van Winkle,
I'm just another visionary bound by hypnosis and sprinkles.

*Author / Jeana Marie Jeffers*

**TAG ME**
**#55**_____

In this realm I perform task out of the ordinary.
I wash the dishes, and return to the real world.

Another time I fed the cat, cleaned the toilet,
And then again I returned to the real world.

Next, I painted a red X on all my neighbor's doors.
And then again I returned to the real world.

Then this world of strange turned for the worse.
I drove my car down a one way street.
What startled me were the honking horns.
But by the oncoming lights I was not fazed.

Quickly I steer the car into an empty lot.
With my palms all sweaty and my heart racing,
I look around and for the first time realize,

# TAGMEWRITE

My roommate was reaping all the rewards.

*Author / Jeana Marie Jeffers*

**TAG ME
#56**_____

I'm a cultural belle of silk in my country.
My tapestry painted like Irises by Van Gogh.
I'm very courteous with my humbling walk.
And I speak of harmony though I do not talk.

*Author / Jeana Marie Jeffers*

**TAG ME
#57**_____

Suddenly I was awakened by this most disturbing commotion going on outside of my bedroom window. As I rolled over to look at my alarm clock I noted the time to be 3:27 in the morning. So, I'm thinking. I know I'm not getting ready to go through another restless Friday night, or in this situation, Saturday, with these two characters.

 My next door neighbors, Mr. & Mrs. Tuggawar, where once again at one another's throat. She was yelling something about him being out all night with his stank tuna fish smelling girlfriend. And he was yelling back at her about not keeping her appointment with the shrink for her paranoia. They both sounded like they were crazy to me, especially since it was way too early in the morning to be up yelling about some fish and chips. And as to why they were outside, and right below my bedroom window announcing to the entire world, that they both had some serious issues is beyond my comprehension.
It seems like nobody really appreciates anymore, what it means to keep your business behind closed doors.

Well the disturbance lasted for about 15-30 minutes. There were shoes flying across the lawn. Golf clubs were used to break out every window in Mr. Tuggawar's Ford Explorer. Then there was some hair pulling and some screaming. No it wasn't Mrs. Tuggawar. Then she ran into the house and came out with a revolver not sure of the caliber because by that time both myself and Mr. Tuggawar vanished clean out of sight.

## May 3, 2013 — Jeana Marie Jeffers

I don't know where he went with them broken out windows, but I ducked down and crawled underneath my bed. And that is where I stayed for the entire night, for I did not see any reason to get shot over their stupid fight.

When the sun came up I crawled out from under the bed after falling asleep. But I kept to my knees, crawling to the other side of the bed to see what time the clock said. The clock read 9:01 which means that after I laid there for several hours in a panic, because of the continuous silence it must have finally lulled me to slumber.

I then crawled out into the hallway, and it was from that vantage point that I took the risk to stand up. Surely Mrs. Tuggawar must be calm by now.

So, I stepped into the shower,
Then I did my thing for an hour.
Then after that I got dressed.
Risk leaving to go have breakfast.

I decided to eat at the Nearby Diner,
Then saw Millie with a big old Shiner.
Gave her a hug fearing she wasn't ready yet,
She cried and said he's going to change,
I said you want to bet.

Then we left the subject alone,
I ordered bacon, eggs and black coffee to carry home.
Then after paying for my order and I was about to exit the diner door,
Up jumps a gunman from the 4th table yelling everyone hit the floor.

So once again I'm confronted with this madness, and have to lay my butt right back on the floor. Though I dare not do anything stupid like scream, or go off, because all this crazy stuff keeps happening and end up provoking this man. So like everyone else with good sense and was already lying on the floor I dropped once again.

Out of curiosity I glanced over at the gunman watching him demand from the cashier all the money. She hands it all over to him minus any resistance. But as soon as the man turned around to run out the door I closed my eyes tight in fear that he might panic and shoot all of us for being an eyewitness. But all he apparently wanted was the money because he ran out that door so fast and never looked back once.

# TAGMEWRITE

Then we all looked at each other wondering if it was safe to get up. But the manager who gave us the all clear ran out the door yelling police, police stop that man I've been robbed.

Then the police officers that where just pulling up to the diner taken off in their squad car in same direction as the gunman but when they returned they said he got away.

So we all lined up to tell our individual versions as to what taken place at the time of the robbery to the officers. The only thing told that matched was the fact that the diner was robbed.

Finally leaving the diner and heading home with my cold coffee and food. Along the way I take in the sights.

There's a gang war going on avec beaucoup de heat.
There's paraphernalia hitting every corner of the streets.
There are children starving from greed and neglect.
The elderly are wondering what ever happened to respect.

TO EVERYBODY EVERYWHERE, THIS IS ENTIRELY TOO MUCH! I HOPE THAT YOU HEAR ME! LET'S PUT AND END TO ALL THIS -----. Beeeeeeeeeeep.

*Author / Jeana Marie Jeffers*

**TAG ME**
**#58**_____

I was part of the pronouncements, it was good.
And temporarily separated from my Brother,
But it was only by a daily division of twelve.

Unlike him, I do not suffer from low self esteem.
For I always keep my lantern set on high beam.
But it was Brother who made my world so bright.
He said to me with his deep dark voice.
I will be one thing and you can be the other,
So I chose to be the one our Father would call Day.

*Author / Jeana Marie Jeffers*

**TAG ME**
**#59**_____

Frenchie - Well as our great mentor already explained.
We came on the scene with the money makers.
Obie - No we didn't.
And as usual you have misinterpreted what she said.
When we started entertaining there was no money involved.
Frenchie - No you're wrong.
We held our very first performance in the early 1600's.
And I specifically recall there being some money changers.
Violie – That last statement is correct but only according to that era.
But your first statement is all the way wrong.
Most of us were making melody at the time of the Chronicles.
And at that time as Obie stated, there was no money involved.
We performed out of respect for the King.
Frenchie – Who is telling this story?
Obie – You are! But you're telling it all wrong.
You need to get your facts straight.
Glockie – Obie I think you need to stop blowing so much hot air,
And let Frenchie finish hanging himself.

Interviewer - Hold on,
Do YOU always dispute with one another like this?
ALL TOGETHER -YES.
Violie - Arguing is the only possible way,
We can give a great performance.
Glockie - So we agreed to disagree.
That way we can get all that negativity out of our systems.
Frenchie - Then the beautiful interviewee sitting right before us,
Obie - Our reason for existing don't leave that out,
Frenchie - Right, we owe our very existence to that TAG.
Therefore when we get on that stage,
We are confident that we are going to do her proud.

*Author / Jeana Marie Jeffers*

# TAGMEWRITE

**TAG ME**
**#60**_____

Well I'm glad that's over.
So now I guess it's my turn to speak.

I have not a prejudice bone in my body,
Being that my bi-racial family are black and white.
Coming from a long line of poetic musicians,
I'm able to synthesize my harmony day and night.

I'm strikingly talented and do love traveling abroad,
Being accompanied by the versatile woodwind family,
And the powerful sound of our best friend the amazing brass.
Smile Frenchie and Obie.
Then we have the percussions that do me competitive justice.
Play on Glockie.
YOU Bad Mamma Jamma YOU!
And last but not least we have multiple strings.
Just look at how polished she looks.
When she plays, every single stroke comes out clean.
Take your bow Violie.

So just like our mentor, I'm proud of them too.
The audience claps and anticipates our every whistle.
They keep me on my toes for when it's time to blend in.

ALL TOGETHER – We love you too! Solo.
Frenchie – Especially after you deliver your keynote address.

Mentor – Don't slight yourself Solo, I'm proud of you also.
Interviewer – wiping tears. Me too,
Now!
How about you joining the rest of them,
And give us a little performance.
Solo – Sounds good to me.
Frenchie – Let's get ready. It's time to make love.
Violie – Let it go Obie.

*Author / Jeana Marie Jeffers*

May 3, 2013  **Jeana Marie Jeffers**

**TAG ME**
**#61**_____

Your outlook on life is distorted.
I know this because I see something different.

Mary, you see a woman filled with sadness.
What I see is a sheep that will help turn the world around.

Peter you see yourself as a stud with the strength of Hercules.
What I see is a man in need of a reality check. But there's hope.

Vashti you see a lady with the entire world rotating around you.
What I see is vanity, needing to change her ways or get dumped.

David you see yourself as a man unworthy of forgiveness.
What I see is a great leader who will stand by his fellowman.

So EVERYONE, check YOURSELVES out daily.
That way you won't come to me being something you are not.

*Author / Jeana Marie Jeffers*

**TAG ME**
**#62**_____

WOW!
What a drag.
These cheeks of mines could use a face lift.
Though I'm not actually referring to those little cherry blossoms of mines,
But about that old guy over there mimicking me with his back out of line.
It's quite possible he would still be physically fit, if like me,
He had munched within his diet on more leaves and greens.
Oh well, you live and you learn.
Let me fly over there and see what my little sister Kadid is up to.

*Author / Jeana Marie Jeffers*

## TAG ME
**#63**_____

Huff, Huff, Huff, Huff,
Whew, something is definitely wrong with this picture.
Why are those stalkers chasing after me?
Is it because they crowned me king of the jungle?

Huff, Huff, Huff, Huff,
Hey what is that over there?
It looks like a temple.
Maybe I can find somewhere to hide.
But quick I know those stalkers can't be too far behind.

Huff, Huff, Huff, Huff
Oh great there are two more of me at the top of the stairs.
Hey you two I would not stay out here in the open like this,
Because there are 10 men and 10 women headed this direction,
And they all are carrying rifles and I think they want to celebrate.

Hey!
Did you hear what I just said?
We need to go find a good place to hide.
Look partner,
(SLAPPING THE IDOL ON THE BACK)
Oh no!
(NOW RUBBING THE IDOL SURFACE)
Aaaaaaaaaaaaaaaaa!
What have they done to you?
They have turned you both into golden statues.
I think I'll go inside and take a quick tour of this shrine circus.
Oh no!
This place is worse than I thought.
Everywhere I turn,
They have imprisoned some poor creature in a shell skin made of rock.
I can't stay here!
There is nothing but still life here.
This must be what is really meant by Animal Kingdom.
So now who's going to worship the ground I walk on?
Yoo-hoo stalkers I'm in here.

*Author / Jeana Marie Jeffers*

**May 3, 2013** — **Jeana Marie Jeffers**

**TAG ME**
**#64**_____

I appear to be experiencing some sort of quiz-optical attraction,
But why for my lens are trained to ignore the world around.
Yet trapped in my mind's eye is this immense diamond-like image.

I imagine owning this beauty with my eyes wide open on lock,
While caressing the gem of my life from the opposite side of glass,
I then rub my pupils hoping that gesture will snap me out of this trance.

Then the proprietor steps in the pathway of my hypnotic view,
His lips move and the words that disturb me are,
Would you like to come and gaze from the inside?

What is wrong with him?
Why would he step into the world of the absurd?
Doesn't he realize that if I lose my focus I might risk lost of sight?

So because I'm hooked,
My lips motion with the return of a silent response,
NO. I want to linger here a little while longer and just stare.

*Author / Jeana Marie Jeffers*

**TAG ME**
**#65**_____

FRED – Ok everybody let's play this game,
And describe this tag with letters A-Z.
If you miss, or your description don't make sense,
You're OUT.
The last person to stay alive wins.
So, I'm going to start us off.

FRED
A - Absorption
WILMA
B -
BARNEY

# TAGMEWRITE

C -
BETTY
D – Dino

BARNEY
Betty honey how in the world did you come up with Dino?

BETTY
Well he is one of us isn't he?

FRED
Ok, I'll let that pass this time Betty.

BETTY
Thanks Fred.

FRED
Ok whose turn is it?
Oh it's on me right.
E - Essential

WILMA
F – Flintstones

FRED
Ok!
Wilma both you and Betty are making the clues to obvious.
One more response like that and you're both out of the game.

WILMA
Oh Fred.
You're taking all the fun out of the game.
I thought you would be proud of me for using our last name.

FRED
Uh Huh!
Moving right along,
Barney my main man it's your turn.

BARNEY
With all these unnecessary interruptions coming from you Fred,
I forget what letter we're on.

FRED
G! G!

BARNEY
Laughing,
A key, key, key!
Ok don't pop a blood vessel.
G – Generic

FRED
Good one Barn.

BETTY
H – Hormones

FRED
That's awesome Betty.
I – Iron

WILMA
Umm let me see.
J – Jujube
And don't you start criticizing my answer Fred.
Do your research I did not make that name up.

FRED
Grumbles, this is just like when we play scrabble,
She always has to show off.

BARNEY
Laughing,
A Key, key, key!
K – I don't dare say Phylloquinone or Fred will have a fit.
Kefir

BETTY
L – Lecithin

FRED
Umm

# TAGMEWRITE

M –
Umm

WILMA
What the matter dear are the responses getting too complicated?

FRED
No! I just need to think.

Jeopardy theme plays in the background.
M – Mr. Slate.

WILMA AND BETTY OBJECTING
No, No, No,

BETTY
You didn't like it when Wilma said Flintstones
Or when I responded with Dino,
You even threatened to oust us out of the game.
So your use of Mr. Slate should not count either.

WILMA
I agree with Betty Fred.

FRED
Ladies, ladies, ladies,
Come on let's be fair.
Didn't I give you another chance?

BARNEY
OK Fred,
We give you another chance to give another clue.
But if you mess up this time, you're OUT!
Laughing,
 A key, key key!

FRED
Ok,
M – Magnesium

BARNEY
Nice come back.

WILMA
N – Niacin

BARNEY
O – Omega 6

BETTY
P – Peppermint

WILMA
Nice one Betty.
I just love the power of peppermint.
It helps my digestive system.
Helps to get rid of my heart burn,
Brought on by you know who.

FRED
Alright that is enough yickety, yacking.
Let's get on with the game.

WILMA
OK,
It's on you.

FRED
R – Riboflavin
Now deal with that!

WILMA
S – Sage

FRED
I'm not even going to question that,
With a response like that,
It is obvious that it is getting close to dinner time.

WILMA
WHAT EVER…………..

BARNEY

# TAGMEWRITE

T – Thiamine

BETTY
U – Uncle Tex

FRED
Betty no matter how much I appreciate that response,
YOU'RE OUT!

BETTY
Ha, Ha, Ha
I don't care,
I just could not leave Uncle Tex out.

FRED
V- Valerian

WILMA
Fred you're cheating,
There is no way I'm convinced that,
You came up with that response all by yourself.
Gazoo where are you?

FRED
Wilma honey it's just a game.
And I'm insulted that you would even think,
That I would stoop to something so lame.

WILMA
Grumbling,
Ooh I could just spit.
W – Hanna & Barbera
Oh!
Now see what you made me do.

FRED
I'm sorry honey,
But you lose.

BARNEY
Laughing,
A key, Key, Key

X - Xylitol
FRED
Umm
I was certain that,
Barn would not come up with anything.
Y -
Hold on,
I know it.
Piss, Gazoo, Gazoo.
I need you buddy.
Come to my rescue.

BARNEY
I'm waiting Fred.

FRED
I got nothing.

BARNEY
I win!
Yahoo, game over!
No, in the words of my best friend,
Yabba
Dabba
Do!

And the final two responses are,
Y – Yucca and Z – Zink

*Author / Jeana Marie Jeffers*

**TAG ME**
**#66**_____

Oops that's incorrect,
Let me try it again.
They say if at first,
Well you know the rest,
Get rid of that!
Blot it out you said?
Correct!

# TAGMEWRITE

I'll provide you with a clean slate.

*Author / Jeana Marie Jeffers*

**TAG ME**
**#67**_____

I enter the hotel lobby hands shielded with latex.
The Manager directs me to the secured room, 202 to be exact.
Once there with my keen eye, I scan the room for any trace evidence,
What I see is unfamiliar little specks of broken glass embedded in the carpet.
Unfamiliar because nothing in the room was a perfect match,
Though I had a hunch the glass was unknowingly left behind by our suspect.

He or She tried to clean up the place, but did so in a moment of haste.
And, after processing the tiny particles under the microscope,
I realize that broken glass left behind, comes from the lens of binoculars.
But the housekeeper reported that there is nobody to investigate,
Though the chalk outline left behind tells a different story.
So I dusted her for fingerprints, because she seemed to be withholding the evidence.
But after several hours of interrogation held in the conference room of the Hotel,
And performing a thorough examination of her deep pockets,
We came up empty handed.
There was just not enough tangible evidence,
That we could use against our prime suspect.

So once again we return to room 202 hoping to confiscate another possible clue,
Only this time we got lucky.
One of us had decided to channel our thoughts beyond the perimeter.
We had overlooked searching the 2$^{nd}$ floor storage closet.
Realizing that when we first apprehended this whimsical beauty,
The vacuum cleaner that she had in her possession,
Since it came up clean,
It was used as a tactical measure to throw our investigation off course.
Therefore buying her some time to return to the real cleaner,
Dispose of the incriminating evidence,
And make a clean getaway.

May 3, 2013    **Jeana Marie Jeffers**

So what we ran into was a locked closet that we had to get the manager to unlock.
Inside were several cleaning items including two not one vacuum cleaners.
So we emptied out the contents of both,
But there was nothing but a few dust particles inside.
So we turned them over only to find that our housekeeper had made a costly mistake.
There were traces of broken glass trapped in the brushes of one vacuum roller bar.
Some of the glass was stained with the blood of our victim.
We had her now. All that was left to do was to make her spill her guts inside room 202.

But if you're curious as to how we knew it was she.
Who else had the opportunity to vacuum prior to removal of the corpse?
And the weapon of choice being that it was binoculars can only mean one thing.
That she was using them to spy on the Hotel resident's between the two buildings.
No doubt she transported them inside of her cleaning cart.
But as to motive, he must have returned to this room and caught her in the act.

*Author / Jeana Marie Jeffers*

**TAG ME**
**#68**_____

They only asked for forty,
But I said I'll give you fifty.
Then the voice within me said,
That's too much!

They wanted a little recreation,
But I said I want a lot.
Then the voice within me said,
That's too much!

They offered me a healthy diet,
But I said I'm use to grease.
Then the voice within me said,

# TAGMEWRITE

That's too much

They told me to drink more water,
But I said no we need more booze.
Then the voice within me said,
That's too much!

They labeled me an extremist.
I said you are absolutely right.
Then the voice within me said,
That is what you might be,
But I'm just the opposite.

*Author / Jeana Marie Jeffers*

**TAG ME**
**#69**_____

I'm wonderfully made even if I'm not all there.
Some have less and others have new repairs.
But it seems to be those with, living in despair.
Calling those without handicapped, that's unfair.

Especially since their coping mechanism is norm.
With help they appreciate being able to move on.
And to those caring for me from the day I was born,
You'll reap rewards for not treating me like a thorn.

*Author / Jeana Marie Jeffers*

**TAG ME**
**#70**_____

Hey poppy, you sure put a whole new twist to fill it to the brim.
What you doing running around looking like Speedy Gonzalez?
I could ask the same question but you look more like Roy Rogers.
Wait! I don't think you completely understand how to Jone.
You telling me that I look like Roy Rogers that's a real compliment.
Well I guess it is all according to how you hear it. Correct?
You were trying to poke fun at me because of how I look.
And I was poking fun at you because you want to be me and missed.
What I'm wearing is a classic and what you're wearing is an imitation.

May 3, 2013  **Jeana Marie Jeffers**

My people made this to serve a good purpose and we wear it proud.
I suggest you stop joning and be proud of the vaquero you're wearing.
Happy trails to you.

*Author / Jeana Marie Jeffers*

**TAG ME**
**#71**_____

Ok let me call up my girls,
It's time for a celebration!
No, too much excitement,
That's a dead giveaway.
But who cares,
God has called us to peace.
Hallelujah!
F-R-E-E-D-O-M

*Author / Jeana Marie Jeffers*

**TAG ME**
**#72**_____

*This story is not about insults.*
*It is just a story to make YOU think.*

As soon as I turned eighteen I was out of the house.
That was the moment I had waited for my entire life.
Always taking orders and following parental rules.
Feeling hopelessly lost and totally misunderstood.

But I knew that if ever that day would come,
I would walk out that door and I would never look back.
And that is exactly what I did, now time to share the facts.

I know you're wondering how an eighteen year old survived.
You will have to read to the end because it's possible I died.

Though I was a city girl the place that I grew up was slow pace.
But I had always dreamed of one day moving to the Big Apple.

# TAGMEWRITE

So that is where I ran to live out my fantasies, at a much faster pace.

Again how would I survive, moving way out there?
Well, I had taken up a trade in High School.
Then I went online to search for a position in that field.
But it had to fit my needs, which was location, location, location.
And Voila!
There it was an opening in my field and located in New York City.

I was confident that I would have no problem landing the position.
And why not, I'm talented and believe that dreams do come true.
And since every single thing was falling perfectly in place,
I knew that my time had arrived so I did not hesitate.

I packed only what I needed and that wasn't very much.
Then I embraced the photo of my parents and said, Goodbye.
It had to be that way because any other path would have been prevented.

I arrived in New York on a Thursday morning.
That was the longest bus trip that I had ever taken and I was exhausted.
So, I was very much in need of a shower and a nice soft bed.
I walked up to the window clerk and asked for directions.
I handed him a piece of paper with an address.
The address was where this twenty two year old named Von resided.
Von had moved away from my hometown to Queens about 3 years ago.
And we decided to keep in touch.
She had a small apartment in Queens,
And she had invited me to come and stay with her until I got on my feet.

To survive Von worked as a stripper.
But I don't judge, in fact I totally agree with the saying,
TO EACH HIS OWN!
The point is we were as different as night and day.
I was shy, not much of a socialite but I was curious.
Von was a party girl, loved to entertain and adventurous.
Hence, I knew it wouldn't be long, before I would move on.

After about 4 months that is exactly what I did.
I could no longer put up with all of her late night guests.
And many mornings waking up to find the apartment a total mess.
Therefore, to maintain our friendship I moved.

## May 3, 2013 — Jeana Marie Jeffers

I wasn't making enough money on an entry level journalist salary.
So I had to move to a place that would be within my budget.

I moved in a house with many rooms for rent.
This time I had to share both bathroom and kitchen with 4 other occupants.
The bathroom situation was somewhat a problem,
But I pretty much ate in my bedroom.
My bedroom, I loved the sound of that.
Behind those four walls I felt right at home.
Unlike before, I shared that space with no one.

No more having to sleep on the hideaway bed,
That I shared with 2 miniature felines.
I guess because I was home more so than Von,
They just became attached.

And no more sleeping in Von's bed,
Whenever she wanted to confiscate mines, or hers,
So that she could party or get busy.

But that is the past and I'm now moving forward.

So in my little four cornered room is where I lived for the next 3 years.
Not being able to afford to move, for as of yet,
I had not received a substantial pay increase.
And because of those late night classes,
That I was taking to try and excel in my professional journalist field,
I had to keep a very low spending profile.
But it wouldn't be long before the rest of my dream would come to life.

There was a story that I very much wanted to cover.
It centered around a serial killer that every 1st Tuesday of the month,
He would strangle a female victim inside their homes.
Then he would leave them propped up at the dining table,
With a pink silk scarf tied around their neck.
He became known as the 1st Tuesday Strangler.

The strangler had been apprehended.
That is how we knew of his gender.
And my boss who was just as curious as I, wanted to know,
What his motives were for the killings?

# TAGMEWRITE

Why the pink scarf?
Why he left them sitting up straight at the dining table?
And why the 1st Tuesday was so significant?

I personally wanted to know how he gained access.
Especially since the women were warned,
To stay off the streets after a certain hour if possible,
Or at least if WE had too, not to go out alone,
And not open our doors to any unknown strangers.

None of them had anything in common
So did he know his victims?

Well if I was ever going to make it in this business,
Then I needed a break so that I could prove myself capable.
That would mean I would have to come from behind the desk,
And step out there in the world to investigate.
Loving It!

So out of the blue, my boss Mr. Staples placed me in charge.
Well it wasn't so much out of the blue.

I woke up on the wrong side of the bed and decided to throw a tantrum.
That was one of the items packed in my suitcase when I moved to New York.

It was time to upload my confidence.
So, in the privacy of Mr. Staple's office,
I merely brought to his attention that I had something more to offer,
Than just sitting behind a desk and cleaning up everyone's mess.
And that I was starting to feel used.
If he truly liked my journalism skills,
Then he was going to have to consider opening up for me another door.

Now!
Out of the blue,
He said you're right!
I have an interview scheduled today at 11:00,
And it just so happens that our strangler,
Has a special request.
He will only share his story with someone new.
So I'm placing you in charge of this cover story.

May 3, 2013    **Jeana Marie Jeffers**

I trust you to get the facts,
And I know Currie that you won't let me down.

I was flabbergasted.
Isn't that something, you can be confident and surprised at the same time.

Well off I went to gather all the facts.
The man behind bars had only agreed to interview with me.
That must be a sign.

The interview was very startling.
Some things he said, though bizarre,
Just did not fall completely into place.
But because this was my golden opportunity,
I made the puzzle pieces come together as if working towards a Pulitzer.

While I was typing those win me a complete place of my own words,
I could feel the changes in the air,
And hear the sweet sound of success tickling my ears.

Yes that article did as I suspected.
It opened up many more doors.
I was now on the road to success.

Mr. Staples allowed me to cover many more stories.
I proved to be an honest, hard working competitor.
So, he placed me second in command in case of his absence.
And he also gave me a handsome raise up front in profit.

I'm living the dream,
Now just 21 and doing my own thing.

I decided to celebrate by going on a shopping spree.
I moved on up like the Jefferson's, and purchased a condo with a balcony.
And guess where?
You know it! New York City baby!
I picked out some furniture some new clothes, shoes, changed my hair,
Started wearing make-up, pedicure, manicure, you know, the works.

I started eating stuff like caviar,
Drinking the good stuff like Bordeaux.

# TAGMEWRITE

But there was one problem,
After 5 months of fame,
I realized that I hadn't made any real friends.
It was time to step out of my shell and let someone in.

But the problem was where?
I didn't want to be picked up by someone at a bar.
That sounded cheesy.
Besides I wasn't looking for a one night stand.
I was looking for someone to call friend.

So just like everything else that has taken place in my life,
Came together at the right time, I decided to let
That part of my dream, to be loved schedule itself too.

And wouldn't you know it, right on time,
I met a guy at the corner market,
Two weeks after I buried the thought.

He was the perfect gentleman.
He treated all women with respect.
And no he wasn't a flirt, he just was packaged right.
He was smart, funny and never put on any airs.

The first time we met,
He said that he had been watching me for some time,
But with everything going on in the news,
With the 1st Tuesday Strangler, he was afraid that
With him being a stranger that he would spook me.
Therefore, he was waiting for the right moment to approach me.

I said watching me, watching me from where?
And if you've seen me why haven't I seen you?
He said. Though I live around here,
Every Tuesday I ride the subway into Queens to visit my father.
After spending most of the day with him,
I would head back and see you getting off the train.
The first time I noticed you was when this elderly man stumbled,
And you reached out quickly and caught him before he fell.
But you didn't stop there, you went the distance,
And grabbed his hand, then you walked him to safety.
Every since then I could not stop thinking about you.

May 3, 2013 **Jeana Marie Jeffers**

I saw something good in you and wanted to get to know you.
So when Tuesday rolled back around,
Not only did I enjoy spending time with my father,
But, now I looked forward to seeing your face every Tuesday.

I was very impressed with him.
In my opinion this was the beginning to a perfect friendship.

For the next two months we exchanged intimate secrets about each other.
Being that he worked out of his home,
Much of our time together was spent at his place.
Then one of his Tuesday visits he taken me to meet his Father.

It was perfect. Because as a token of his appreciation,
Mr. Staples arranged for me to have the day off.

Marco's father, a very nice man, was confined to a bed.
But what I did not know until the day I met his dad,
Was that Marco's mom was alive because he never spoke of her.

At the time of the visit she was there.
She was very pleasant and they seemed to get along well.
So I inquired later as to why he never mentioned to me about his mom.

He said, well we don't always see eye to eye when it comes to Dad.
I'm sure that she wants the best for him,
But I would like for her to respect how I feel about him too.
But that is never going to happen,
Even before Dad ended up in the condition he is now,
She has never taken me serious or even understood me.

I can relate to that.

He said, with all that you have told me,
That I can believe.

I tell you what, enough of this talk about mother.
She will be leaving town this weekend, with a friend of hers.
So I'm going to give her a break and stay with Dad,
Until she returns home on Tuesday morning.

# TAGMEWRITE

So how about we have dinner at your place,
And I'm going to provide the meal,
And do all the cooking.

I responded. Sounds like a perfect evening to me.

We are making headway now.
I've been to his place.
I've met both his parents.
And now he is stepping over into my world.
Yeah!

Well now it is Tuesday,
And the entire day all I could think about was tonight.
This was going to be the news story to make headlines,
"I Found A Friend."

Since everything had been wrapped up early for the day,
And Mr. Staples was out of town on business.
I decided to leave someone else in charge and go home.

I arrived home about 4pm and quickly took a shower,
And changed into something more comfortable but sexy.

Dinner was scheduled for six.
But I wanted to make sure that the atmosphere was right.
So I selected the music and made sure that my scent was everywhere.

Marco arrived right on time.
He rang my buzzer and I cautiously inquired as to who was calling.
He responded back with, it's me!

I laughed behind the buzzer not wanting to risk insulting him.
Then I buzzed him in.

When I opened the door,
There he stood with a very large but lovely basket and a smile.

I then invited him in and closed the door behind him.
Then said hello, and he said, "Hi", then kissed my lips.
I then said ooh whatever you have in that basket smells delicious.
That is when he started naming off the menu.

## May 3, 2013 — Jeana Marie Jeffers

He said, I know it has been a long time,
Since you've had a real home cooked meal.
So I have fresh greens out of my garden,
Homemade mashed potatoes,
Just the way you like them with lumps.
A beef roast smothered in gravy and onions,
And some home style hot watered corn bread.
Then of course, I brought with me some red wine.
"We will talk dessert later."

I laughed at his flirtatious manners.

By the way he said.
"You look good in that pink off the shoulder lace handkerchief dress.
I like that color on women."

"Thank you baby, you look good to me too in all that black.
Now let's eat I'm starving."

The meal was fantastic.
We sat there eating, talking,
Laughing, and enjoying one another's company.
When dinner was over, together we washed and dried the dishes,
Then we sit down on the sofa with another glass of wine to talk.
By that time, I really wasn't too excited about talking,
I was concentrating on getting to the next stages of sealing our friendship.
But out of appreciation I listened.

I had loaded the mp3 player with a variety of music.
At that particular moment Boney James version of Stop,
Look, Listen to your heart, was playing.

Marco was telling me a story about his Mother that rung strange.
He said. Mother is the cause of Father being bed ridden.
She does not think I know about it,
Because dear old Mom, has been living in total darkness for a very long time.
But I think she is slowly coming around.
You see I had to do something to get her attention.

What are you saying Marco?

# TAGMEWRITE

Don't you know?
It was you who did the interview.
I know that whatever that impostor told you,
Could not have had any ring of truth.
But yet you chose to print a lie and let that man rot in jail,
For crimes that you know within your soul that he did not commit.
Why? Self Interest, that's why.

I stood up and said.
Marco you're scaring me.
I think you better leave now.

Then Marco said. Sit Down!
And if you try to scream for help,
I will go off the grid and cut your throat.

He continues.
My Father worked as a Public Accountant,
And had spent most of his time traveling,
But he was getting older,
I had gone away to college,
Therefore he decided that he needed to spend more time with Mom.
So he cut his schedule down to only traveling 1 week out of the month.

That is when Mother every 1st Tuesday of the month for the past 6 years
After Dad left for his business trips, started having her week long affairs.
It could have started way before then,
But Dad did not start getting suspicious until about a year and a half ago.
That is when the pink silk scarf showed up.
Dad recognized the manufacturer.
It was made and designed in Paris France.
So he knew that she had either been to France without his knowledge,
Or someone else gave her the scarf,
And because of the cost he was sure it was a man.
Not that another woman would not spend that much for a gift,
But Mother was very secretive about the scarf and treasured it.

So to prove his theory,
Dad had scheduled his trip for the second week of the month,
But he never mentioned to Mom about the change.
He wanted to catch her in the act.

## Jeana Marie Jeffers
*May 3, 2013*

Soon as he left for the pretend trip,
Mom was out the door and headed for Long Island.
Dad followed her to a man named Stanley Staples house.

What! Mr. Staples!
But he is married.

True, but as they say when the cat's away the mice will play.
My Mom and Staples have been lovers for a very long time.

Wait he is out of town now and due back tomorrow.
Your Mother came back today.

Now you're catching on.
The affair stopped after the first three deaths.
They were both convinced that the strangler was me.
But then you ruined that.
And then about 2 months ago,
The affair started again.

That was when you met me.

Bingo!
Well since you never asked,
Allow me to tell you what happened to Dad.

My Father waited all night for Mom to come out,
But that never happened.
He wanted to go up to the door and knock,
But once the lights went out,
All he could do was sit there and cry.
So he drove off in his emotional state of mind, and drove his car off a cliff.

What you see now is the results.
When I came home from school,
Dad told me everything.
So I did some investigating of my own.
And that is how I found out the truth about my dear old Mother.
So her punishment is to take care of Dad for the rest of his or her life.
And now she has to live with the guilt of having a serial killer for a son.

# TAGMEWRITE

*Marco puts on his gloves at the time of making that statement.*

"So you killed those women to punish your Mother?
But how could you condemn them to death for what she did?"

They were all tested just like you!
When I took them, same as I did you, to meet Dad,
Just the same as you, they never inquired about his condition.
But, what they were curious about, and you as well,
Was why I never mentioned to them about my Mother?

Go figure!
There lies a Man in a pitiful state,
But your concern and theirs too, is my disloyal Mother.

"But we had no idea."

"As to whether or not you knew is not the point.
You knew enough to inquire, so why not about him?"

So are you saying that if they had asked about your Dad,
That they might still be alive today?

I won't know the answer to that question until it happens.
But the way I see it every last one of you are just like Mom,
SELFISH!

That's not true in my case.
Remember the old man that you saw me helping.
Don't that count for something?

Currie baby, please.
You just wrote a story that condemned an innocent man to death.
So you helped that old man to ease your own conscience.
Because of guilt, that is why Mom is helping Dad.
But she hasn't learned anything about loyalty.

What makes you any better than us Marco,
You lied to me and no doubt all the others,
Just so you could avenge your Father.

That's where you are wrong.

## May 3, 2013 — Jeana Marie Jeffers

I never once lied to any of you.
See you're confusing not telling you everything with a lie.
Don't that sound strange to you?
Don't answer that.
All of a sudden you're an expert on lies.
You adjust how you view things according to your situation.
The man lying on death row meant a profit.
Then the man standing before you right now,
You accuse of lying with false reasoning,
But in reality you're trying to bargain with me for your life.
That's SAD.

You poor thing you started off wrong from the beginning.
You bring nothing but pain to every life that you touch.
Unlike me, you had a very good Mother,
But you turned your back on her,
And never ever wrote her a letter to let her know you were OK.
That is a major failure on your part, and that is going to cost you.
And today is the 1st Tuesday of the month.
But you consider yourself privileged.
Because you are the only one that I ever told the whole truth,
And you're going to carry it with you to your grave sweet baby.
And dear old Mom is going to know for sure that she created a monster.

I was now facing the dragon and I wanted my Mommy.
I wanted to tell her that I was sorry for hurting her and Daddy.
Marco, please, no.
You said you loved me.

And I do my darling.
But I love my Father too.
And my first place loyalty belongs to him.

I try to run for the door and I scream.
But Marco places his hand over my mouth and drags me to the dining room table.
I try hard to fight back, but he over powers me.
Then he reaches inside the basket and pulls out a pink silk scarf.
Then he slowly and firmly pulls the scarf tight,
And then strangles the life out of Mademoiselle Currie.

# TAGMEWRITE

He then props her up in the chair at the table,
Combs her hair and wipes away her tears,
Kisses her goodbye, then exits apartment 607 with his basket.
*The exit song on the mp3 is Lalah Hathaway's "Breathe."*

But as he is walking down the hallway,
The lady in apartment 610 opens her door and say,
Excuse me sir.
Did you hear someone scream?

No ma'am I'm sorry I did not.
Maybe you heard a scream on the TV down the hall.
Or could it be your mind playing tricks on you?

No I'm sure the scream I heard was real.

Marco said as he slowly approached her.
It's possible.
But I think you made a _____.
DOOR CLOSING
Locks CLICK, CLICK, CLICK

*Author / Jeana Marie Jeffers*

## TAG ME
#73 _____

I am born but they dare not disclose my face,
For when I die they sacrifice and fear thy living.
Although legally I'm confirmed by written deeds,
Yet I'm sealed with marbled eggs and pagan trees.

I'm uncertain if I should be considered as habitual,
Though being lit is more desirable than mourning.
And I feel heightened when jumping the broom,
 But why must 24 be restraint for bride and groom?

Is it fact that I practice the whitewashing of graves?
Or am I the one being detained at the bonded store?
Whatever the case I smuggled but all in good taste.
Because I really love YOUR countries style and place.
C'est pourquoi je dis merci beaucoup pour la variété.

May 3, 2013

# Jeana Marie Jeffers

*Author / Jeana Marie Jeffers*

## TAG ME
## #74 _____

I speak every known language of people far and near,
But greetings are my favorite response to the listening ear.
And with my long stretched neck way in the clouds I hear,
A single tear drop of success that is loud and clear.

Though in my depressions I listen to all those lost in fear,
At times becoming aggravated, causing things to disappear.
That type of internal disturbance I wish not to reappear,
For the devastation can last, for many a year.

But after hours of anxiety is shouted way up in the sky,
I pajama up, though never do I really mean to say goodbye.
For even during the darkest hours do I mimic with repetition,
Though never am I negligent as to your uttering benedictions.
So if you feel the need to cross the waters and escape,
Then come and lay it on me, because I'm an open gate.

*Author / Jeana Marie Jeffers*

## TAG ME
## #75 _____

The immoral woman will bait the fool with her heart,
And then lure her curious nibblers to shallow waters,
A place designated to inject them with topical disease.
And that is why her heart is comparable to flaxy Ode to me.

The stalker will target their game as personal property,
Leaving a cereal trail that leads to the vanishing forest,
A place designated to swing baskets from shady trees.
And that is why their schemes are comparable to flaxy Ode to me.

The one going into battle will snatch you from behind,
Then drag you throughout the four levels of your mind,
A place designated to explore while pondering the sea.

# TAGMEWRITE

And that is why their conquests are comparable to flaxy Ode to me.

The Heavens have opened to bucket drop a limited time,
Collecting their harvest from the pastures of humankind,
A place designated to gift those hearts that are complete.
And that is why the Reign in Heaven is comparable to flaxy Ode to me.

Peter, Andrew, James and John engaged within this trade,
But they made the perfect sacrifice to follow the Christ,
To a place designated for his honorable bride class to be.
And that is why they had success with their catch, in flaxy Ode to me.

*Author / Jeana Marie Jeffers*


**TAG ME**
**#76**_____

I'm not so pretty lying underneath the skin,
But the ones who marked me said look again.
They seem to be obsessed with discoloration,
And claim to be the Co-Founders of intimidation.
But the pressure to stop the movement is great,
So after the pain and swelling leaves and I dissipate,
The next time I show up it won't be by mistake,
Therefore I advise you to keep awake.

*Author / Jeana Marie Jeffers*

**TAG ME**
**#77**_____

Comparatively more pleasant to hear are words selectively sweet.
Like nectar I do soften the tongues of the wise and of the discreet.

I'm often an endearing term whenever lovers do favorably greet.
Then we celebrate over hot tea with me added as a special treat.

But be careful, don't overindulgence or I'll sicken your happy feet.
Be cautious like Samson who from the carcass of the lion did eat.

May 3, 2013   **Jeana Marie Jeffers**

All this talk about me has made me tired so time for me to sleep.
But remember to prevent decay, to brush and rinse your teeth.

*Author / Jeana Marie Jeffers*

## TAG ME
#78 _____

Come, ride the elevator and see what it's like atop of my world.
Just step inside those double doors and push level one zero four.
Now, take a look around, and poetically recite what it is you see.

As I slide in circular motion by way of your connecting skywalk.
I see infinite purple mountains that take me on a mile high ride.
I see beyond the leaves of your bigger than life majestic limbs,
The blinding rays of sun with a proposal for peace to be-wed.

I taste and smell fresh air because it is much cleaner than below.
I see stretched for miles a flowered quilt of assorted meadows.
I hear laughter and echoing smiles ringing in every nearby town.
The view up here is so lovely that I don't ever want to come down.

And you don't have too!
You can build your nest up here with us.
Our roots are strong.
We can stand our ground against any quakes.
We don't have problems with flooding.
And we have our own guaranteed 3000 year term life insurance policy.

*Author / Jeana Marie Jeffers*

## TAG ME
#79 _____

It's peaceful.
The walls are filled with joy and laughter.
No one crosses the line and invades the others privacy.
Love is the foundation.
Trust is the bonding tool.
And EVERYONE is welcomed.

# TAGMEWRITE

Girl you need to stop tripping!
You know that isn't the right description.

It's off the chain.
The walls are filled with grumbling.
Everybody is all up in your business.
But it is LOVE holding that crazy place together.
TRUST takes one look at those dysfunctional faces and runs.
ENTER AT YOUR OWN RISK!
But I have to warn you.
You might get shot for TRESPASSING.

Now out of the two descriptions,
Which one do YOU believe branded the saying that there is no place like it?
I'm putting my money on number 1.

*Author / Jeana Marie Jeffers*

**TAG ME**
**#80**_____

You know it is taking forever for that dough to rise.
Just wait it will happen.
Boy I sure wish that the summer would hurry and come.
Just wait it will happen.
How many hours left before the sun comes up?
Just wait it will happen.
You know it has taken forever for there to be a black President.
Just wait it will happen.
You know I don't believe that Armageddon is ever coming.
Just wait it will happen.
You know if you would daily apply a tiny bit of me,
You would be surprised at how much easier waiting could be.

*Author / Jeana Marie Jeffers*

**TAG ME**
**#81**_____

The giant lord of the beanstalk,
He crushes me for his two ton barrel of lukewarm root beer.

May 3, 2013  **Jeana Marie Jeffers**

Like Mystique I shape change to an ice castle,
Just so the wicked Queen can chant mirror, mirror.
I'm a tube of Preparation-H for the Abominable Snowman,
And a cozy dream sickle for Mr. Freeze and his beloved woman.

*Author / Jeana Marie Jeffers*

**TAG ME**
**#82**_____

Hey Bubbles what you doing?
Well I'm pretending to try and master a new trick.
Why do you have to pretend?
Because if you haven't figured it out already Dolly,
There is a connection between performance and reward.
And these humans think that they are teaching us new tricks.
When in reality it is we who are training them to do our bidding.
You see rolling in the water is something delightful to them.
But it was my ancestors from long ago to discover spiral swimming.
It's just something that we do, but these people think it's something new.
So last week when they gave me a demonstration,
I did everything within my power to keep from laughing.
I attentively watched my trainer as if I knew nothing,
Then I gave her this puzzled look as if her instructions were unclear.
Though I was only waiting for her incentive to appear.
 And there it was tasty morsels for my palate.
So, I gave in to the command of a roll, and then I rolled for her again.
I was trying to win her heart, of which that I most certainly did.
And now she wants me to jump through hoops,
I guess she doesn't realize that I'm a breaching expert,
Although that is a good thing because I don't want her feelings hurt.
So I'm going to practice a little more then I'm going to get my reward.
I do say that this is the good life,
I don't have to hunt or sneak up on my supper anymore,
All I have to do is satisfy my employer.
Oh and I'll be shooting my very first video this week.
Along with cutting a brand new CD set to MP3.
They seem to be very intrigued by my resonating sound.
Who knows I might like some of my other cousins,
Land a movie career.
Dolly then said.

# TAGMEWRITE

Watch out now!
Soon they might have to deflate your ego.

*Author / Jeana Marie Jeffers*

**TAG ME**
**#83**_____

My heart is blue from the lost of you,
Flying in my lonely space;
Until over the cuckoo's nest I flew.

But I'm trying my best to emotionally heal,
By sharing with others how rejection can make one feel,
Therefore I sung about those memories in baritone fairytale.

From the very moment you entered this world,
Not once did you consider giving our love a whirl,
Yet I treasured your worth like a precious pearl.

And when you escaped with your life from the family of knots,
I waited for your return, as my heart for you went flip flop,
But you drifted far away to be captured by the claws of Camelot.

Then once again I saw the possibility of us bonding,
For the friends of Camelot snubbed you with stern reprimanding.
Although that form of rejection did not affect your fine standing.

For me though your trials pushed you even farther from my life,
You ended up falling in love with a prince that made you his wife.
Then you grew wings and changed your name to Umm.

Who Are You?
And that is how rejection makes one feel,
It hurts you to the point of where you just want to forget the real.

*Author / Jeana Marie Jeffers*

**TAG ME**
**#84**_____

Oh my goodness as Shirley Temple would say,

**May 3, 2013** — Jeana Marie Jeffers

Too many spicy foods have upset my tummy.
I feel so bloated that I could just let it all go,
But all this gas could do some serious damage.

Whew!
Things are starting to really heat up in here,
I might have to take the entire bottle of Tums.
Burp.
Wow that feels a little better.
Burp.
Oh, oh I hope I did not get any on you,
Because that little bit just might burn.
Burp.
I think my tummy is starting to settle,
And hopefully the next time my insides won't explode.

*Author / Jeana Marie Jeffers*


**TAG ME**
**#85**_____

The sound of a penguin when courting his mate is a hoot.
When his newly-wed returns about 65 days later they sing.
We imitate the animal gestures by silent finger motions.
Some wag their tails, twitch their ears or flap their wings.
Don't forget the wolf high upon a cliff howling at the moon.
Who is she calling or is this some type of special warning?
There's the greeting of our giant floppy eared elephants.
They say lay it on me baby and give me that warm snot.
Wow, what a nice expression of love.
And then there is US.
The HUMAN
When you use me, you either build up or tear down.
And often we choose the latter.
You use me with your facial expressions, body gestures, etc.
And best of all you use me in over 400 different dialects.
Now that is something pretty about me.

*Author / Jeana Marie Jeffers*

# TAGMEWRITE

**TAG ME**
**#86**_____

I hear you calling me from the Buoyancy Vaughn View,
The words are come pass time current passes through.
Accepting your invitation like an Angel I hover above,
Then I photo shoot your blue body that fits like a glove.

I wish my heart were like yours so I too could sustain life,
Just seeing you in motion can help anyone sleep at night.
As I sleep dreaming about your adaptable circumstances,
I discover the sunken secret how you dissolve substances.

So the very next day I gear up to dive into your deep fold,
After about a minute of contact the body ceases to be cold.
I then dive for the bottom with plankton brushing my sides,
Then you place in my hand treatment and then say goodbye.

As I return above your surface I breast stroke the final mile,
Clutching the remedy that you gave and doing so with a smile.
I thank you for the lesson in love and will guard it forever,
Until we meet again my friend you are a wonderful treasure.

*Author / Jeana Marie Jeffers*

**TAG ME**
**#87**_____

I'm a thrill seeker,
And I enjoy living life on the edge.
I've taken many a risk,
Some of which at times, has confined me to a bed.

But, my life seems dull and boring,
When there are no extreme challenges to face.
So, whenever I put on my ARMOR
I feel, strange though it may seem, SAFE.

*Author / Jeana Marie Jeffers*

**TAG ME**
**#88**_____

May 3, 2013  **Jeana Marie Jeffers**

It's the perfect fantasy world,
Where you can whisper a dream and it appears.
If troubled times come calling,
I can put on hold all thoughts until the morning.
Then when you open your eyes,
The channel is changed to a brand new program,
That only permits good thoughts to share our space.
But if ever those wicked seeds try to take control,
At your command I will uproot them from the soul.
For my spyware can protect our fantasy home,
But, you must choose what to feed the salvation dome.

*Author / Jeana Marie Jeffers*

**TAG ME**
**#89**_____

I am a stalker that goes by the name of Aquila.
I rule from a lofty throne with much wisdom.
A blood sucker and a victory symbol of la guerre.
And a professional pilot that soars through the air.

*Author / Jeana Marie Jeffers*

**TAG ME**
**#90**_____

I know dear,

I'm filled with your favorite creation embodied with 50-70 percent.
I'm writing because my mouth is streaming with resourceful events.

To get things flowing, in May, they have planned several casino trips.
I'm looking forward to just cruising along with the weight of the ship.

The middle of June, lumberjacks have scheduled a logrolling contest.
Weeks of preparation, for some vandals left beer bottles in my chest.

And lastly in July, we're going to recreate the adventures of Huck Finn.
Naturally they'll symbolize me as the mode of escape for him and Jim.

# TAGMEWRITE

I'm so excited, and can't wait to see you.
But for now I'll hold on to the memories
Of hearing your stories while bathing you.

Au Revoir!

*Author / Jeana Marie Jeffers*

**TAG ME**
**#91**_____

Work hard work,
An army of soldiers
Stacking their cabinets
In case of famine

Queen of the nest
Though never bossy
Widowed much too soon,
Yet, extinction is no threat.

Bona Fide Resume
Excellent Role Models
Industrious
Organized planners
Self Motivated
Weight Bearers
Pulling more than
So get with the program.

*Author / Jeana Marie Jeffers*

**TAG ME**
**#92**_____

You know something is definitely wrong with you.
Unlike your twin who is always so pleasingly sweet,
You will sever the head of a donkey if he tries to speak.
Now I don't want you to take what I'm saying literally,
I'm just speaking in general.
But I read crazed letters in your eyes that spell mutilation,

May 3, 2013    **Jeana Marie Jeffers**

I believe a direct result from your most recent amputation.
But you must dispel from your mind those wicked thoughts,
Before it is too late and you end up being forever lost.
And put behind you all those horrible deeds of Glen Falls,
And accept that there is no more unity for you two at all.

*Author / Jeana Marie Jeffers*

**TAG ME**
**#93**_____

Shake your boom boom shake your boom boom,
Come on Serpentine shake your boom boom with me.

You know what? You're impossible.
Everyone else is shuffling to a triple beat,
And you're over here shaking your boom boom.
But this is not the time to shake our booties with this crowd.
If you want to be accepted,
You got to get on the dance floor and step twice but quick,
Then step slower than the other two,
And then kick your way to acceptance.
Just keep right on doing that and we've got it made.

What!
 I did not come here to try and fit in.
That's Ok I did.

Oh! One more thing,
We are not doing any of those crazy moves
From Saturday Night Fever either.

*Author / Jeana Marie Jeffers*

**TAG ME**
**#94**_____

I became an overnight sensation because of my many eyes.
More productive than the English Channel,
Child you better recognize.

# TAGMEWRITE

I really get turned on whenever I hear my audience clap.
But I'm not too thrilled with your resolution for fine tuning,
I thought the whole idea was pretty whack.

You might think so, but a good choice for a sitter I am not.
Since I can be very addictive in the area of entertainment,
Therefore my suggestion is that you clap again Sherlock.

*Author / Jeana Marie Jeffers*

**TAG ME**
**#95**_____

I'm so glad that I waited for this moment.
Even though all is not perfect,
If I had ran ahead of my indecisive heart,
Perfection would be the portrait wanted.

But how did I outgrow my unrealistic fantasies?
I had to sit down and take a good look at myself,
Then decide if I could be good to someone else.
Though I could only fill my head with future lies.

So for years I processed all of my expectations,
Then I learned on site a few to do's or not to do's.
Then I put them all together and prayed for help.
And then I was able to move on, to a better song.

*Author / Jeana Marie Jeffers*

**TAG ME**
**#96**_____

We are about to pull off the greatest heist in all the universe,
We are going to steel 5,000 diamonds worth 25,000,000,000,
Straight out of the night deposit box of the Stellar Space Building.
And the best part about this caper is that no one will ever miss them.
You know why?
Because there are billions and billions and billions and billions and,
Ok, we get the point.
They have billions and billions.
Exactly!

May 3, 2013  **Jeana Marie Jeffers**

They have so many that they can't even keep account of them all.
Ok, so what's the plan?
Ok pay very close attention.
Tomorrow night at midnight,
The four of us are going to board the shuttle,
But to avoid any suspicion,
We will enter one at a time 10 minutes after the other.
We need to bring enough rope to string 1,250 diamonds each.
Rock, you TAG the Ash collection.
Stone, you can TAG the Kesil's.
Jewel, you're assigned to TAG the Kimah's.
And I will be responsible for TAGGING the Mazzaroth collection.
Now once we enter that shuttle and push the start button,
We have exactly five days to complete our mission.
So there is no turning back.
I think you mean there is no coming back.
Count me out.
Me too,
Me also,
What's the matter you afraid of getting burned?

*Author / Jeana Marie Jeffers*

**TAG ME**
**#97**_____

What's my type?
I can answer that question without even thinking about it.

We both have to be on the same EXACT spiritual plane.
That way he's not changing for me, and I'm not for him.
But we see the need for change according to the will,
Of He who brought us together.
So he'll get rid of the ritual salt, and I'll get rid of the crushed pepper.
Because remember, we both now walk in the same name.

Also!
He needs to be big and strong, with extremely tight muscles.
But humble, peaceable, not intimidating,
Or one who loves throwing his weight around.
So he'll have to lose the cloth, and I will have to lose the attitude.

# TAGMEWRITE

Because remember, we both now walk in the same name.

I'm not picky about his ethnicity,
I'm intoxicated by his body.
And I will choose him over Tarzan to swing in the Jungle with any day.
Because remember, we both now walk in the same name.

*Author / Jeana Marie Jeffers*

**TAG ME**
**#98**_____

We're ALL in training and want to be good at what we do.
Roll call.
Jackets and Vest – READY
Boats and Dinghies – READY
Doctors, EMT'S, Firemen, Officers – READY
Divers – READY
Centurions – READY
The Elderly – READY

Umm – Excuse me sir.
But how does that last call fit in our training exercise?
Haven't you ever heard Soldier the old saying take a lesson from the wise?
MAKE A DIFFERENCE.

*Author / Jeana Marie Jeffers*

**TAG ME**
**#99**_____

Ok this is going to blow your mind.
It's a story about a man in a motorized wheel chair,
And we're going to call him Willie.
Well one day Willie was out visiting a few friends.
He made his first stop at the corner barber shop.
The barber shop was always a place of comfort.
Willie could tell a few jokes and laugh a little.
After about an hour or so, Willie said his goodbyes,
And out the door he rolled in the direction of the market.
He had about $15 in his pocket and wanted to buy,
Bread, Hotdogs, and a small package of ground beef.

## May 3, 2013 — Jeana Marie Jeffers

Those were the items that he had written down.
He loved chili dogs and was going to have them for supper.
He was a thrifty shopper and knew the bread would cost
About a $1, the hotdogs about $2 because they were
Made with turkey, and the ground beef about $1 for
It was a markdown item because of the expiration date.
So $4 was all he expected to spend on his dinner.
Then after paying exactly what he had calculated,
Willie rolled on down the street to the drug store.
He needed to pick up two prescriptions.
One was for the pain in his lower back and legs,
The other was for his blood pressure.
The cost for both prescriptions was a co-pay of $4 each.
So now he is left with only $3 and Willie like most of us,
Who loves kicking back to an ice cold Beer,
Asked the lady behind the checkout counter,
To ring him up a 40 ounce of Old English.
After paying for that he was now left with a $1.
Before leaving Willie told her a joke.
Why?
Because that was something she had grown accustomed to.
Then he rolled away laughing with his Bread, Hotdogs,
His Ground Beef, Med's and a 40.
Willie had rolled about two blocks in the direction of town,
Crossed the busy intersection at 36th and Illinois,
Was just about at his apartment on 36th and Meridian,
When this guy jumped out of nowhere,
Pointing a gun in Willie's face and demanding money.
Willie said,
Man I ain't got nothing but a dollar.
The guy said, give it to me.
Willie reached in his pocket and pulled out his last dollar,
Then he handed it over to the armed man.
Then the man said,
What else you got?
Willie said just a meal and something for me to drink.
The armed man took that from Willie too.
Willie said that is all I have left to eat.
What am I suppose to do for food?
The guy said,
What's more important right now, your life or your big belly?

# TAGMEWRITE

Willie said well naturally I'm going to choose my life.
The guy said, then shut up and hand over that other bag.
Willie said man no not that,
I need these for pain and to keep my blood pressure under control.
The man said, I'll tell you what.
I will give you the blood pressure medicine,
Because I'm sure after this you're going to need them.
But I'm keeping the prescription for pain.
I'm sure that I can get something for them off the streets.
But I'm also taking your wheel chair.
My grandmother could use a nice chair like this.
So he takes Willie by the arm and drags him to the ground.
Then he sits in the wheel chair and rolls away,
With the Bread, Hotdogs, Ground Beef, Pain Medicine, 40 and chair.
Now I think I should tell you how Willie ended up in the wheel chair.
One night he was coming home from work and had just got off the bus.
As he was crossing the street,
A car sped around the corner and struck him.
The driver fled the scene leaving Willie for dead.
But as you can see, Willie is a survivor.
So after about 15 minutes had passed by,
Because Willie maintained a perfect record in punctuality,
Two of Willie's friends started to inquire as to Willie's whereabouts.
When no one could give them a satisfactory response,
They took off in search of their dear friend.
It did not take them long at all to find Willie.
Being that Willie had previously informed them where he was headed.
They found Willie around the corner on 36th street.
He was sitting there with his back up against a sycamore tree.
As they approached him, Willie just looked at them and laughed.
He said a funny thing happened to me today.
I got wheelchair jacked.
Both men looked at each other strangely,
Because they knew whatever happened wasn't a laughing matter.
But after about 30 seconds the humor started to sink in.
So they like Willie started laughing their heads off too.
When all three men finally composed themselves,
The two friends stood on opposite sides of Willie,
Then they each placed on arm under Willie's arms,
And their other arm under Willie's legs and carried him home.
Once there one of the friends called to report the incident.
When the police officer arrived,

**May 3, 2013**    **Jeana Marie Jeffers**

Willie was grateful that it was someone he knew.
Confident that justice would be served.
The officer wrote down every single detail,
Not missing a beat.
Then before he left,
He told Willie not to worry that tonight dinner was on him.
Everyone in the neighborhood knew that Willie was just an ordinary man,
And that he lived on a fixed disability income.
At times to make extra cash he hustled or collected a few beer cans to sale.
So the police officer just did not feel right just leaving and doing nothing.
But out of respect for Willie and all that he had been through,
He dignified Willie by saying,
Which do you prefer, Chinese, fried chicken with potato salad, or chili dogs?
Willie said, Man those first two choices sound real good,
But my heart was set on those chili dogs.
Then chili dogs it is.
Then before the officer closed the door,
Willie jokingly gave the officer a tip.
He said Man I truly respect what you do,
But you keep alert out there because these perpetrators today are
_____.

That night Willie watched basketball with his friends,
They all ate chili dogs and enjoyed an ice cold beer.
And the very next day Willie's wheelchair was returned by the officer.
And the thief was caught red handed selling Willie's prescription on the corner of 38th
Stupid! But that is not it.

These perpetrators today are _____.

*Author / Jeana Marie Jeffers*

**TAG ME**
**#100**_____

They finally made the perfect model for me.
And they graded you A, high honors indeed.
All you needed to pass by me was 100 percent.
But you went and doubled the score, EXCELLENT!

I see not obsolete in your future or saying farewell.

# TAGMEWRITE

Since your birth you have shaped an amazing trail.
One that prevented me from cheating on you,
Neither did I have a longing to be driven by another.

So as I'm perching in the comfort of your leather.
I smile at me in your mirror for having it together.
Then I think. What if I'm becoming a lover of Material?
Then back to Germany you'll go, and I'll keep Spiritual.

*Author / Jeana Marie Jeffers*

**TAG ME**
**#101**_____

Around the entire globe people suffer from me,
As we sit up all night eating popcorn and watching TV.

And it was I, pacing the floor with the spouse of Queen Esther all night.
And if Nebuchadnezzar had no dream, he would not have given me light.

The Doctors and shrinks say I exist because of consistently poor habits.
But if that were the source then why do they treat all of YOU just like lab rabbits?

Oh Well!
Whatever the cause I'm glad the Redacteur stayed awake to include my story,
Since I see no reason why,
Yawn,
You're just about finished lady,
Now complete that last rhyme.
Why ALL those other TAGS should recieve ALL the glory.

*Author / Jeana Marie Jeffers*

May 3, 2013  **Jeana Marie Jeffers**

## TAGMEWRITE ALPHABETICAL LISTING

THE FOLLOWING ARE THE GAME CHOICES. JUST BECAUSE THEY ARE NUMERICALLY NUMBERED LIKE THE POETIC BODIES, DO NOT GET CONFUSED AS TO HOW THEY MATCH. THAT WOULD MAKE THE GAME NO FUN. THERE ARE NO DUPLICATE ANSWERS BECAUSE I WROTE THEM ALL WITH THEIR VERY OWN SPECIAL TAGMEWRITE IN MIND. ENJOY!

1. ACID RAIN
2. ADVENTURER
3. ALMOND
4. ANDES MOUNTAINS
5. ANTS
6. APPLE
7. ARTHRITIS
8. BANK
9. BASKET CASE
10. BEAR
11. BILL OF RIGHTS
12. BRAIN
13. BRUISE
14. BULLY
15. BUTTERFLY
16. CAPTIVATED
17. CHINESE BUFFET
18. CHOCOLATE
19. CONFIDENT
20. CONFUSED
21. CRIME SCENE
22. CROWN
23. CUSTOMS
24. DANGLING PARTICIPLE
25. DIVORCED
26. DRAGNET
27. DRAMA
28. DREAMS
29. EAGLE
30. EARTH
31. EARTHQUAKE
32. ERASER
33. FEVER

# TAGMEWRITE

34. FRIENDS
35. FROG
36. GOSSIPHER
37. GRASSHOPPER
38. HEART
39. HOME
40. HONEY
41. IGLOO
42. INNOCENT
43. INSOMNIA
44. KILLER WHALE
45. KIMONO
46. LADY CARDINAL
47. LANGUAGE
48. LIFE PRESERVERS
49. LIGHT
50. LION
51. MARGE SIMPSON
52. MARRIED
53. MERCEDES BENZ
54. MIRAGE
55. MIRROR
56. MISTAKE
57. MODERATION
58. MUHAMMAD ALI
59. MUSIC
60. PARADISE
61. PATIENCE
62. PIANO
63. RESPECT
64. ROSES
65. SCANDALOUS
66. SEQUOIA TREES
67. SKELETON BONES
68. SLEEP WALKER
69. SNAKE
70. SOAP
71. SOMBRERO
72. SPIDER
73. STARS
74. STEEL MAGNOLIAS
75. STILETOOS
76. STORMS
77. STUBBORN
78. SUMO WESTLER
79. SUNKEN TREASURE

| | |
|---|---|
| 80. | SYMPHONY ORCHESTRA |
| 81. | TABLE |
| 82. | TEARS |
| 83. | TELESCOPE |
| 84. | TELEVISION |
| 85. | THE BIBLE |
| 86. | THE CONGA |
| 87. | THE DEAD SEA |
| 88. | THE FOUR WINDS |
| 89. | THE HUMAN BODY |
| 90. | THE MARRIAGE OF A WASHER AND DRYER |
| 91. | THE MOON |
| 92. | THE OCEAN |
| 93. | THE RIVER |
| 94. | THE SUN |
| 95. | THUMBELINA |
| 96. | TIME MACHINE |
| 97. | TUNNEL |
| 98. | TYRANNOSAURUS REX |
| 99. | VITAMINS |
| 100. | VOLCANO |
| 101. | ZEBRA |

# TAGMEWRITE

## TRIBUTE

**PLEASE TAKE TIME TO READ THE FOLLOWING TRIBUTE**

WWI July 1914 – November 1918
WWII 1939 – 1945
VIETNAM - 1959 - 1975
Atlanta 1979 - 1981
911 - 2001
Volcanic Eruption Hawaii 1983 & 1990
Genocide 1994
Columbine 1999
Tsunami Malaysia 2004
Hurricane Katrina 2005
Earthquake Haiti 2010
Earthquake Chile 2010
Gulf Oil Spill 2010
Earthquake & Tsunami Japan 2011
Southside Explosion November 2012
Newtown December 2012
Boston Marathon April 2013
Iraq & Afghanistan
And there are so many other dates to bring to life.

Because I have included these events at the conclusion of the game, I feel that it is absolutely necessary for me to give everyone an explanation. But first, I want to apologize if any feelings get hurt, that's not my intentions. I do not, and I repeat do not view any of these CATASTROPHES or senseless acts of bloodshed in any way as a game. Losing a loved one is very hard. So I wanted to take time out to keep those beautiful memories alive.

Some of the dates mentioned, naturally I was not born when they taken place but the overall thought to come away with, is that in one way or another they have affected our lives and continue to do so.

The one that I have carried with me the longest happened in Atlanta in 1979. Though I did not know any of the innocent victims personally, I was truly saddened by the story and all the lies surrounding it. And now I'm going to

**May 3, 2013** — **Jeana Marie Jeffers**

carry even more, but I'm willing because my arms are wide open to every single one of YOU beautiful people that I view as my neighbor.

So I want all families around the globe to know that everywhere they turn there are people out there who do share their tears and truly care.

Earthquakes, Hurricanes, Tsunami's etc. they are all natural disasters that are beyond our control. But all these other violent acts are unnatural though they both leave us with many unhappy tears. But stay strong.

"Just a little while longer and the wicked one will be no more" - Psalm 37:11

So again, all around the world I send YOU my dearest sentiments and heartfelt love.

Now, take 30 minutes or however long you desire for YOURSELVES and do something nice to make YOU or SOMEONE happy.

Much Love
*Jeana Marie Jeffers*

# TAGMEWRITE

Jeana Marie Jeffers

# TAGMEWRITE
## 101

## MUTANT POETRY
# THE BOOK

May 3, 2013  **Jeana Marie Jeffers**

**TAG ME**
**ACID RAIN**

Your collapsible source of shade will be incomplete,
 As they search for my cure throughout many holes.

But, I'm complicated and conceal myself amid the fog.
Traveling great distances and breaking international laws.

Then after my precipitating values have both intermingled,
They settle like dewdrops giving birth to aquatic disasters.

In the past, my treatment was an enormous sliver of lime.
But, for future reference,
Quit smoking the pipes and everything will work out just fine.

*Author / Jeana Marie Jeffers*

**TAG ME**
**ADVENTURER**

I'm a thrill seeker,
And I enjoy living life on the edge.
I've taken many a risk,
Some of which at times, has confined me to a bed.

But, my life seems dull and boring,
When there are no extreme challenges to face.
So, whenever I put on my ARMOR
I feel, strange though it may seem, SAFE.

*Author / Jeana Marie Jeffers*

**TAG ME**
**ALMOND**

While strolling through my popcorn like meadow I blow upon you my ring,
Daydreaming of the times that you need me more so than when you do not,
Calling your name requesting that you meet with me at the first sign of spring,
Though it is customary for us to wait until the harvest, therefore you cannot.

# TAGMEWRITE

Yet, delightful is how I feel when dreaming of you consuming my peach like smile,
But nothing can compare to our copied scent of roses saturating the air,
As we roast alongside the campfire honey dipping our first born child,
Being careful not to draw undo attention, fearing others might come and stare.
So be patient my love, soon the time will come for you to enjoy the full aroma,
Therefore behold from the mountain top a beautiful orchard filled drama.
Because from there, it's impossible to miss a single pink blossom come to life,
As the stage down below appears to be covered with what looks like white ice.
So stay focused, and don't lose sight of our nature valley performance,
For we hold true to the promise of meeting all your needs, with an abundance.

*Author / Jeana Marie Jeffers*

## TAG ME
## ANDES MOUNTAINS

I speak every known language of people far and near,
But greetings are my favorite response to the listening ear.
And with my long stretched neck way in the clouds I hear,
A single tear drop of success that is loud and clear.

Though in my depressions I listen to all those lost in fear,
At times becoming aggravated, causing things to disappear.
That type of internal disturbance I wish not to reappear,
For the devastation can last, for many a year.

But after hours of anxiety is shouted way up in the sky,
I pajama up, though never do I really mean to say goodbye.
For even during the darkest hours do I mimic with repetition,
Though never am I negligent as to your uttering benedictions.
So if you feel the need to cross the waters and escape,
Then come and lay it on me, because I'm an open gate.

*Author / Jeana Marie Jeffers*

May 3, 2013  **Jeana Marie Jeffers**

**TAG ME**
**ANTS**

Work hard work,
An army of soldiers
Stacking their cabinets
In case of famine

Queen of the nest
Though never bossy
Widowed much too soon,
Yet, extinction is no threat.

Bona Fide Resume
Excellent Role Models
Industrious
Organized planners
Self Motivated
Weight Bearers
Pulling more than
So get with the program.

*Author / Jeana Marie Jeffers*

**TAG ME**
**APPLE**

They said it was I, who played a role in the first sin,
But they don't know they weren't even there.

I don't like speculation it's bad for my reputation,
And to accuse me without evidence is very unfair.

The second lie told, was that I practiced medicine,
And that lie turned Jekyll into Hyde and me into sauce.

So, I demanded after witnessing their perjury for a retrial,
For it is not I who lied, what they are spreading is false.

But the judge said SILENCE! Order in the court!
Then said, Are you, or are you not, the pupil of the eye?

# TAGMEWRITE

*Author / Jeana Marie Jeffers*

**TAG ME**
**ARTHRITIS**

Day One
Crack
Oh LORD I can hardly move.

Day Two
Crack
Oh LORD this day is worse than the first.

Day Three
Crack
Oh LORD can you help me I'm stuck.

Day Four
Crack
Oh LORD
Thank you!
For today I only feel it in my knees.

Day Five
Crack
Oh LORD my fingers are stiff,
Can you strengthen me so I can open this jelly jar?

Day Six
Crack
Oh LORD
Thank You!
For it is a beautiful day

Day Seven
Crack
Oh LORD
Thank You!
I am not going to complain,
For tomorrow I have to start the process all over again.

*Author / Jeana Marie Jeffers*

**TAG ME**
**BANK**

I protect you from those rainy days,
And put back for vacations on the way.
There are times when predators clock me,
But those violators provide no necessity,
For my institution is built on trust,
And will charge the fee of handcuffs.
Though some might escape to a Netherland,
Stealing from me is no mere walk in the sand,
Because I have a close friend living by the shore,
And wouldn't you know it,
She bears the same name as me,
And with interest will collect ALL lost currency.

*Author / Jeana Marie Jeffers*

**TAG ME**
**BASKET CASE**

You know something is definitely wrong with you.
Unlike your twin who is always so pleasingly sweet,
You will sever the head of a donkey if he tries to speak.
Now I don't want you to take what I'm saying literally,
I'm just speaking in general.
But I read crazed letters in your eyes that spell mutilation,
I believe a direct result from your most recent amputation.
But you must dispel from your mind those wicked thoughts,
Before it is too late and you end up being forever lost.
And put behind you all those horrible deeds of Glen Falls,
And accept that there is no more unity for you two at all.

*Author / Jeana Marie Jeffers*

**TAG ME**
**BEAR**

Oh Boy!

# TAGMEWRITE

Yawning
Here I go
Time to take my winter nap
And during the course of my slumber
I will dream about what we share in common
The dipping of our fingers in the honey jar
What a tasty thrill!
But first I need a piece of bark
To floss that Salmon stuck between my teeth
Let me see
What's next?
Oh yeah!
Time to take a quick shower
In the waterfall right outside my den
That way I'll be nice and clean
So here I go
Entering my nice and peaceful retreat
Placing behind me that nagging female
So here I go
Time to get some sleep
Yawn and Stretch
Goodnight!

*Author / Jeana Marie Jeffers*

**TAG ME**
**BILL OF RIGHTS**

I came in a package of ten,
But oft not honor the written guarantee,
For the battle of controversy is what I maintain,
Still anything else is just a turbulence of memories.

Yet, my three branches continue to grow stronger,
Working night and day to satisfy # ones hunger,
You know the one that considers all of our needs,
Though that reality can only be realized prophetically.

So who if any truly understands my definition of justice,
When so many drastic changes keep standing between us,
All I know is that I must work harder to get it right,
And I will not stop until I hear everyone say ALRIGHT.

*Author / Jeana Marie Jeffers*

**TAG ME**
**BRAIN**

It's the perfect fantasy world,
Where you can whisper a dream and it appears.
If troubled times come calling,
I can put on hold all thoughts until the morning.
Then when you open your eyes,
The channel is changed to a brand new program,
That only permits good thoughts to share our space.
But if ever those wicked seeds try to take control,
At your command I will uproot them from the soul.
For my spyware can protect our fantasy home,
But, you must choose what to feed the salvation dome.

*Author / Jeana Marie Jeffers*

**TAG ME**
**BRUISE**

I'm not so pretty lying underneath the skin,
But the ones who marked me said look again.
They seem to be obsessed with discoloration,
And claim to be the Co-Founders of intimidation.
But the pressure to stop the movement is great,
So after the pain and swelling leaves and I dissipate,
The next time I show up it won't be by mistake,
Therefore I advise you to keep awake.

*Author / Jeana Marie Jeffers*

**TAG ME**
**BULLY**

I think you're fat,
I think that you're ugly,
I hate your guts
Without any rhyme or reason,

# TAGMEWRITE

Your existence makes no sense,
So my goal is to end all the suspense.
But, there is one thing I like about you innocent FOES,
You make it easy to plant inside your minds my WOES.

*Author / Jeana Marie Jeffers*

**TAG ME
BUTTERFLY**

I can be lace across your waist
A camisole where one fits ALL
A charm bracelet or an anklet
A tattoo to be shared with YOU
I enjoy flirting in a field of flowers
Flying with my family of farmers
Musing far above the moth mazes
And met morphing many miracles
Think not hard for I am beautiful
The children loving me chases
The adult awes my colorful oasis
And lastly, I crawl before I walk.

*Author / Jeana Marie Jeffers*

**TAG ME
CAPTIVATED**

I appear to be experiencing some sort of quiz-optical attraction,
But why for my lens are trained to ignore the world around.
Yet trapped in my mind's eye is this immense diamond-like image.

I imagine owning this beauty with my eyes wide open on lock,
While caressing the gem of my life from the opposite side of glass,
I then rub my pupils hoping that gesture will snap me out of this trance.

Then the proprietor steps in the pathway of my hypnotic view,
His lips move and the words that disturb me are,
Would you like to come and gaze from the inside?

What is wrong with him?
Why would he step into the world of the absurd?

Doesn't he realize that if I lose my focus I might risk lost of sight?

So because I'm hooked,
My lips motion with the return of a silent response,
NO. I want to linger here a little while longer and just stare.

*Author / Jeana Marie Jeffers*

## TAG ME
## CHINESE BUFFET

They call me cabbage patch kid, but I look more like Bok Choy.
They call me snow, but I'm a tasty green legume.
I like to soak my feet in water, but I'm not a nut.
According to the character writing about me I'm one of the best tasting beans.
And I'm a magnificent spice that can also be taken as a medicine
Our other cuisinart relatives are Uncle Stir Fry, Papa Pan Fry, and Good ole Grand-Daddy Deep Fry. And don't forget about Aunt Sushi, Momma Wonton and Grand-Ma Rangoon.

*Author / Jeana Marie Jeffers*

## TAG ME
## CHOCOLATE

I am so good to you during times of stress,
Making you forget all your troubles is what I do best.

I am not a masseur or masseuse,
But I can put your palates to good use.

When winter time comes and you need a fix,
You add me to l'eau or leche and mix.

You do me proud by placing me high on the gift list,
And if ever you stop smiling I'll blow you another kiss.

Be good to yourself but indulge carefully,
And always remember that my job is to keep you happy.

# TAGMEWRITE

*Author / Jeana Marie Jeffers*

**TAG ME**
**CONFIDENT**

I want it.
I love it.
Will one day have it!
I need it.
So I grab it.
And now it's all mines.
I'm the proud owner of,
This seize the moment TAG.

*Author / Jeana Marie Jeffers*

**TAG ME**
**CONFUSED**

Ok do I want to go to the store?
Or should I sit here and watch TV?
Did I put those shoes over there?
Where in the world is Marvin?

Wait a minute.
Wasn't it Marvin who told me to stay black?
No what he had said was,
Never mind who cares about what he said.

I'm not sure which side of the track I belong.
And what does that mean anyway?
I've seen a whole bunch of people switching sides.
Either you do or you don't which one is it?

Make up your mind you are taking too long.
That's what Marvin said I'm dead in the head.
Was he serious or was he making a joke?
Oh well I guess I'll go to the store.

*Author / Jeana Marie Jeffers*

May 3, 2013 — Jeana Marie Jeffers

**TAG ME**
**CRIME SCENE**

I enter the hotel lobby hands shielded with latex.
The Manager directs me to the secured room, 202 to be exact.
Once there with my keen eye, I scan the room for any trace evidence,
What I see is unfamiliar little specks of broken glass embedded in the carpet.
Unfamiliar because nothing in the room was a perfect match,
Though I had a hunch the glass was unknowingly left behind by our suspect.

He or She tried to clean up the place, but did so in a moment of haste.
And, after processing the tiny particles under the microscope,
I realize that broken glass left behind, comes from the lens of binoculars.
But the housekeeper reported that there is nobody to investigate,
Though the chalk outline left behind tells a different story.
So I dusted her for fingerprints, because she seemed to be withholding the evidence.
But after several hours of interrogation held in the conference room of the Hotel,
And performing a thorough examination of her deep pockets,
We came up empty handed.
There was just not enough tangible evidence,
That we could use against our prime suspect.

So once again we return to room 202 hoping to confiscate another possible clue,
Only this time we got lucky.
One of us had decided to channel our thoughts beyond the perimeter.
We had overlooked searching the $2^{nd}$ floor storage closet.
Realizing that when we first apprehended this whimsical beauty,
The vacuum cleaner that she had in her possession,
Since it came up clean,
It was used as a tactical measure to throw our investigation off course.
Therefore buying her some time to return to the real cleaner,
Dispose of the incriminating evidence,
And make a clean getaway.

So what we ran into was a locked closet that we had to get the manager to unlock.
Inside were several cleaning items including two not one vacuum cleaners.
So we emptied out the contents of both,

But there was nothing but a few dust particles inside.
So we turned them over only to find that our housekeeper had made a costly mistake.
There were traces of broken glass trapped in the brushes of one vacuum roller bar.
Some of the glass was stained with the blood of our victim.
We had her now. All that was left to do was to make her spill her guts inside room 202.

But if you're curious as to how we knew it was she.
Who else had the opportunity to vacuum prior to removal of the corpse?
And the weapon of choice being that it was binoculars can only mean one thing.
That she was using them to spy on the Hotel resident's between the two buildings.
No doubt she transported them inside of her cleaning cart.
But as to motive, he must have returned to this room and caught her in the act.

*Author / Jeana Marie Jeffers*

**TAG ME**
**CROWN**

Surrounding you with loveliness is my way of protecting you,
Like the thorns blossoming above our heavenly bridegroom.
Though in this honorable system I do wear the golden trophy,
As I lavish gray-headedness with a spruce of fame and glory.

The women in your life bring praise to their beloved families,
Their heads showered with the gems from Jacob's fountain.
If they wear me proud the title will be earned your majesty,
And no one will be able to lift the headdress of your authority.

As for the little ones they want to be footstep followers,
As they mimic me with braided hair and honorable flowers.
Yet with me they will continue to achieve their royal dignity,
As they rise with scepters in hand above educated poverty.

*Author / Jeana Marie Jeffers*

**May 3, 2013** — Jeana Marie Jeffers

**TAG ME**
**CUSTOMS**

I am born but they dare not disclose my face,
For when I die they sacrifice and fear thy living.
Although legally I'm confirmed by written deeds,
Yet I'm sealed with marbled eggs and pagan trees.

I'm uncertain if I should be considered as habitual,
Though being lit is more desirable than mourning.
And I feel heightened when jumping the broom,
 But why must 24 be restraint for bride and groom?

Is it fact that I practice the whitewashing of graves?
Or am I the one being detained at the bonded store?
Whatever the case I smuggled but all in good taste.
Because I really love YOUR countries style and place.
C'est pourquoi je dis merci beaucoup pour la variété.

*Author / Jeana Marie Jeffers*

**TAG ME**
**DANGLING PARTICIPLE**

I'm flying through the air with the greatest of ease,
Departing my verbs, de, de, de, de,
Ooh Weeeee!
Hick Up!
I'm hanging in the air, rah, rah, rah, umm care.
No!
Suspended in the air, oh look, Niagara Falls.
Hick Up!
Ok, that's enough my speech is slurred,
No, Subject Impeded.
Time to get to the other side of this,
Rah, rah, rah, umm trapeze.
Dang!
What's that net?
Ah beautiful rope.

*Author / Jeana Marie Jeffers*

# TAGMEWRITE

**TAG ME
DIVORCED**

Ok let me call up my girls,
It's time for a celebration!
No, too much excitement,
That's a dead giveaway.
But who cares,
God has called us to peace.
Hallelujah!
F-R-E-E-D-O-M

*Author / Jeana Marie Jeffers*

**TAG ME
DRAGNET**

The immoral woman will bait the fool with her heart,
And then lure her curious nibblers to shallow waters,
A place designated to inject them with topical disease.
And that is why her heart is comparable to flaxy Ode to me.

The stalker will target their game as personal property,
Leaving a cereal trail that leads to the vanishing forest,
A place designated to swing baskets from shady trees.
And that is why their schemes are comparable to flaxy Ode to me.

The one going into battle will snatch you from behind,
Then drag you throughout the four levels of your mind,
A place designated to explore while pondering the sea.
And that is why their conquests are comparable to flaxy Ode to me.

The Heavens have opened to bucket drop a limited time,
Collecting their harvest from the pastures of humankind,
A place designated to gift those hearts that are complete.
And that is why the Reign in Heaven is comparable to flaxy Ode to me.

Peter, Andrew, James and John engaged within this trade,
But they made the perfect sacrifice to follow the Christ,
To a place designated for his honorable bride class to be.

And that is why they had success with their catch, in flaxy Ode to me.

*Author / Jeana Marie Jeffers*

**TAG ME
DRAMA**

Suddenly I was awakened by this most disturbing commotion going on outside of my bedroom window. As I rolled over to look at my alarm clock I noted the time to be 3:27 in the morning. So, I'm thinking. I know I'm not getting ready to go through another restless Friday night, or in this situation, Saturday, with these two characters.

My next door neighbors, Mr. & Mrs. Tuggawar, where once again at one another's throat. She was yelling something about him being out all night with his stank tuna fish smelling girlfriend. And he was yelling back at her about not keeping her appointment with the shrink for her paranoia. They both sounded like they were crazy to me, especially since it was way too early in the morning to be up yelling about some fish and chips. And as to why they were outside, and right below my bedroom window announcing to the entire world, that they both had some serious issues is beyond my comprehension.
It seems like nobody really appreciates anymore, what it means to keep your business behind closed doors.

Well the disturbance lasted for about 15-30 minutes. There were shoes flying across the lawn. Golf clubs were used to break out every window in Mr. Tuggawar's Ford Explorer. Then there was some hair pulling and some screaming. No it wasn't Mrs. Tuggawar. Then she ran into the house and came out with a revolver not sure of the caliber because by that time both myself and Mr. Tuggawar vanished clean out of sight.

I don't know where he went with them broken out windows, but I ducked down and crawled underneath my bed. And that is where I stayed for the entire night, for I did not see any reason to get shot over their stupid fight.

When the sun came up I crawled out from under the bed after falling asleep. But I kept to my knees, crawling to the other side of the bed to see what time the clock said. The clock read 9:01 which means that after I laid there for several hours in a panic, because of the continuous silence it must have finally lulled me to slumber.

# TAGMEWRITE

I then crawled out into the hallway, and it was from that vantage point that I took the risk to stand up. Surely Mrs. Tuggawar must be calm by now.

So, I stepped into the shower,
Then I did my thing for an hour.
Then after that I got dressed.
Risk leaving to go have breakfast.

I decided to eat at the Nearby Diner,
Then saw Millie with a big old Shiner.
Gave her a hug fearing she wasn't ready yet,
She cried and said he's going to change,
I said you want to bet.

Then we left the subject alone,
I ordered bacon, eggs and black coffee to carry home.
Then after paying for my order and I was about to exit the diner door,
Up jumps a gunman from the 4$^{th}$ table yelling everyone hit the floor.

So once again I'm confronted with this madness, and have to lay my butt right back on the floor. Though I dare not do anything stupid like scream, or go off, because all this crazy stuff keeps happening and end up provoking this man. So like everyone else with good sense and was already lying on the floor I dropped once again.

Out of curiosity I glanced over at the gunman watching him demand from the cashier all the money. She hands it all over to him minus any resistance. But as soon as the man turned around to run out the door I closed my eyes tight in fear that he might panic and shoot all of us for being an eyewitness. But all he apparently wanted was the money because he ran out that door so fast and never looked back once.

Then we all looked at each other wondering if it was safe to get up. But the manager who gave us the all clear ran out the door yelling police, police stop that man I've been robbed.

Then the police officers that where just pulling up to the diner taken off in their squad car in same direction as the gunman but when they returned they said he got away.

## May 3, 2013 — Jeana Marie Jeffers

So we all lined up to tell our individual versions as to what taken place at the time of the robbery to the officers. The only thing told that matched was the fact that the diner was robbed.

Finally leaving the diner and heading home with my cold coffee and food. Along the way I take in the sights.

There's a gang war going on avec beaucoup de heat.
There's paraphernalia hitting every corner of the streets.
There are children starving from greed and neglect.
The elderly are wondering what ever happened to respect.

TO EVERYBODY EVERYWHERE, THIS IS ENTIRELY TOO MUCH! I HOPE THAT YOU HEAR ME! LET'S PUT AND END TO ALL THIS -----. Beeeeeeeeeeep.

*Author / Jeana Marie Jeffers*

**TAG ME**
**DREAMS**

Hint,
With me you can be anything that your heart desires,
You can be a superhero that comes to save the day,
Where everyone is puffing up your chest with Hooray!

Hint, Hint
But there are many times when I extinguish your fire,
I simply flip the script deflating your chest undercover,
Then you toss, turn, and sweat until you foolishly blubber.

Hint, Hint, Hint
Most of me you forget, but others you dig deeper to hire,
Someone more lucid than thou to X-plicate my true definition,
But to justify their cause, they label me as mere premonition.

Hint, Hint, Hint, Hint and that be four
I'm a speedy Z-mystery for all my fallen subjects to inquire,
Though I'm not to be confused with the story of Van Winkle,
I'm just another visionary bound by hypnosis and sprinkles.

# TAGMEWRITE

*Author / Jeana Marie Jeffers*

**TAG ME**
**EAGLE**

I am a stalker that goes by the name of Aquila.
I rule from a lofty throne with much wisdom.
A blood sucker and a victory symbol of la guerre.
And a professional pilot that soars through the air.

*Author / Jeana Marie Jeffers*

**TAG ME**
**EARTH**

I wonder what it would be like,
If I just up and ejected everyone in outer space?

There would be no more Crime or Injustice.
There would be no scent of Hatred in the air.
There would be no more Starvation or Malnutrition.
There would be no Verbal, Physical or Mental Abuse.
There would be no more Stealing or acts of Violence.
There would be no more Pollution spread everywhere.
There would be no more War of any sort soiling the core.
There would be no more Lies told in white or living color.
There would be no more Forest Fires destroying my seeds.
There would be no more causes of Death used to fertilize my hair.

But wait!
Unless that is the perfect plan, I just can't eject,
All that bad stuff up there in outer space,
For that would not be justifiable or even done in good taste.

No, I need to keep them right here where they belong,
Detained and in my custody,
Then ground them for committing all those major atrocities.

Yes, that is exactly what I'm going to do.
I'm just going to continue right on hanging in there,
And wait on our loving Creator to make me brand spanking new.

## Jeana Marie Jeffers

*Author / Jeana Marie Jeffers*

**TAG ME**
**EARTHQUAKE**

I have a humongous appetite,
That swallows everything in sight.
But only if the scales are right,
Do I sink my teeth in the over bite.

My hunger meter is a built in tremor,
That shakes me like a cold December.
After filling my belly it tries to simmer,
But the after math can be even grimmer.

So before I eat, I always sound an alarm,
Basic instinct warns there could be harm.
And that what comes next is out of the norm,
So flee everyone from the gluttonous storm.

*Author / Jeana Marie Jeffers*

**TAG ME**
**ERASER**

Oops that's incorrect,
Let me try it again.
They say if at first,
Well you know the rest,
Get rid of that!
Blot it out you said?
Correct!
I'll provide you with a clean slate.

*Author / Jeana Marie Jeffers*

**TAG ME**
**FEVER**

My goodness it's freezing cold in here.
No I think you're mistaken it's burning up.

# TAGMEWRITE

No you're wrong it's shivering cold.
No you're wrong I'm sweating bullets
Ok who turned up the heat?
No! Who turned it down?
Oh shut up!
Why don't you both take a chill pill!

*Author / Jeana Marie Jeffers*

**TAG ME
FRIENDS**

I'm there for you when things get at their worse.
I'm even there whenever you need to converse.
When I broke down and had fallen by the wayside,
Both you and I sat together and shared our cries.
And as we look at one another's imperfections,
All we recognize is the same identical reflections.
And we're willing to make the ultimate sacrifice,
So let us etch ourselves a legacy in history for life.

*Author / Jeana Marie Jeffers*

**TAG ME
FROG**

Thanks Doc,
I really appreciate you seeing me on such short notice.

You are quite welcome.
Though I must first warn you,
I have never practiced psychology with anyone of your kind,
But since this month business has been a little slow,
Revamping my venue will do just fine.
So, shall we get started?
What would you like to share today?

GREAT!
So where should I begin?
Ok, Ok!
This is where it all started.
I know you heard about those ten plagues right.

### May 3, 2013 — Jeana Marie Jeffers

RIGHT!

RIGHT!

Well why did we have to come in second place?
Surely with all of us hiding in ovens and all that dough,
One of us could have raced first across that finish line.
But NOOOOOOOOOOO!
You know always a loser never a winner.

No I don't know. But!

Sorry don't interrupt,
That was just a figure of speech.
Anyway…………..
Then it was that kissing thing.
So many women were looking for their prince,
That I had to keep my lips puckered for centuries.
No decades.
Hold it which one is the longest?
Let me see a century has umm 10, 20, 40, 50, 100,
A decade has 10, 20, 40, 50, 100,
Ok for eons of years.
And do you know what everyone of them had the audacity to say,

I'm curious tell me.

Ha, Ha
I like you Doc.
Well they all said - YUK!
Every time I heard it, it just tore my poor little heart to pieces.

Well at least they didn't slap your face.

Ah!
It sounds as if you've been there before.

Back it up!
It's you on the couch not me.

Well, do you want to change?

# TAGMEWRITE

I'm willing if you're willing.
Besides, by now it is pretty obvious that I'm never going to turn into a prince.

No..........
I think I will just keep dealing with my own stack of cards.
What else you got?

How about what they did to us in Biology class and Jurassic Park.

Yes, I get the full picture now.
You must be really messed up.
So this is what I'm going to do for you.
For all your pain and suffering,
I'm going to write you a prescription for OxyContin.
Take two of those at night before you sleep,
Then you call me in the morning,
Ok.

Gee, thanks Doc.
You're the greatest.

Oh! By the way,
The whole time of my visit I want you to know that I was working on Self Control.
But I've noticed that over there in the corner you have a miniature problem with pests,
And since I don't have pockets to carry credit cards or cash,
In exchange for your services I would like to pay you for my visit - SLURP!
Sorry, I thought my offer would go over better if I just gave you a little demonstration.

Private thought.
Umm, he could be useful,
Maybe I need to reconsider the OxyContin therapy.

*Author / Jeana Marie Jeffers*

**TAG ME**
**GOSSIPHER**

I've been accused of talking too much
And some things I say are untrue

And I've been guilty of slander
A breach in the partnership rule
Though I hesitate at times
Thinking before opening my mouth
But the contents within tickle my insides
Until I can no longer contain the reviews

Though I am not to blame
For trifling with your great name
The blame can only fall upon your shoulders
For not being the first to keep your secrets
Especially if you don't want them to be heard
For people like me, tune in to every single word.

*Author / Jeana Marie Jeffers*

**TAG ME**
**GRASSHOPPER**

WOW!
What a drag.
These cheeks of mines could use a face lift.
Though I'm not actually referring to those little cherry blossoms of mines,
But about that old guy over there mimicking me with his back out of line.
It's quite possible he would still be physically fit, if like me,
He had munched within his diet on more leaves and greens.
Oh well, you live and you learn.
Let me fly over there and see what my little sister Kadid is up to.

*Author / Jeana Marie Jeffers*

**TAG ME**
**HEART**

I feel congested because you left me broken.
So I sought out Humpty Dumpty,
To ask how he put the pieces back together.
He said.
First they tried to use reverse psychology.
Yelling Humpty,
Why don't you try and pull yourself together.

# TAGMEWRITE

But that didn't work.
He said.
For my chambers were in total disarray.
Then they tried using some super glue.
But the shape came out totally wrong.
One side was up and the other was down.
So then finally, they took me to see a surgeon.
And what he did I will never forget.
I then said, with a tiny bit of excitement.
Something I haven't felt in a very long time.
Tell me Humpty what did he do, for you?
He said and I mean the surgeon.
Humpy, I have some good news and some bad,
How do you want it?
Humpty said.
Let's start with the bad.
Well this one is so badly damaged,
And there is no possible way to repair it.
But here's the good news.
I'm just going to give you a new one.
Humpty said.
YEAH!
I said.
WOW!
That day I learned two things.
  I was replaceable.
And Humpty was like Frankenstein.
He let the weight of this world make him crack.
To the point of where he needed a new brain.
So I left there with a whole new outlook on life.
Rejecting all that cholesterol bull you feed me.
And unlike Humpty,
  I will always maintain my unique composition.
Because like lovely Aaliyah said,
  I CARE FOR YOU.

*Author / Jeana Marie Jeffers*

**TAG ME**
**HOME**

It's peaceful.

**May 3, 2013** — Jeana Marie Jeffers

The walls are filled with joy and laughter.
No one crosses the line and invades the others privacy.
Love is the foundation.
Trust is the bonding tool.
And EVERYONE is welcomed.

Girl you need to stop tripping!
You know that isn't the right description.

It's off the chain.
The walls are filled with grumbling.
Everybody is all up in your business.
But it is LOVE holding that crazy place together.
TRUST takes one look at those dysfunctional faces and runs.
ENTER AT YOUR OWN RISK!
But I have to warn you.
You might get shot for TRESPASSING.

Now out of the two descriptions,
Which one do YOU believe branded the saying that there is no place like it?
 I'm putting my money on number 1.

*Author / Jeana Marie Jeffers*

**TAG ME**
**HONEY**

Comparatively more pleasant to hear are words selectively sweet.
Like nectar I do soften the tongues of the wise and of the discreet.

I'm often an endearing term whenever lovers do favorably greet.
Then we celebrate over hot tea with me added as a special treat.

But be careful, don't overindulgence or I'll sicken your happy feet.
Be cautious like Samson who from the carcass of the lion did eat.

All this talk about me has made me tired so time for me to sleep.
But remember to prevent decay, to brush and rinse your teeth.

*Author / Jeana Marie Jeffers*

# TAGMEWRITE

**TAG ME**
**IGLOO**

The giant lord of the beanstalk,
He crushes me for his two ton barrel of lukewarm root beer.
Like Mystique I shape change to an ice castle,
Just so the wicked Queen can chant mirror, mirror.
I'm a tube of Preparation-H for the Abominable Snowman,
And a cozy dream sickle for Mr. Freeze and his beloved woman.

*Author / Jeana Marie Jeffers*

**TAG ME**
**INNOCENT**

I entered the corner store totally ignoring the warnings,
For my brother had begged me to stay away from there,
Stating that the people inside were not wrapped too tight.
But this day was different for today time was on my side,
I had 20 minutes to kill until the bus to work would arrive.
So, because I was craving for an ice cold bottle of coca cola,
And that was the only available place to satisfy my desire,
I thought that if I'd be quick about it, I might not get caught,
Especially since no other patrons were inside to finger me.
So I did what I knew to be the correct thing to do,
And that was to approach the man behind the counter,
Doing so with a mild spirit because my day was going right,
I then said. Good morning Sirs, acknowledging security also.
I would like to purchase please a nice cold bottle of Cola.
Then right at that very moment three other ladies entered.
Each of them walked right up to the counter and lined up,
I greeted them all, but none accepted the deliverance.
Then the man behind the counter colored me invisible.
He said to the first woman, how can I be of assistance?
She requested a pack of cigarettes and some chewing gum,
He rung her up, she surrendered her cash, thanked him,
He reciprocated and added look forward to seeing you again.
Then she left and he replayed the scenario of ignorance over.

To the second woman he said, how can I be of assistance?
That is when I said, while trying to remain calm.
Excuse me Sir but I was here first.

## May 3, 2013 — Jeana Marie Jeffers

Can I please get that cold bottle of Cola? I have a bus to catch.
He said. In a minute! The longer it sits the colder it gets.
The security person snickered from behind his newspaper,
And the second woman rolled her eyes at me as if I was wrong.
Then she said to the man behind the counter,
I need some aspirin for my splitting headache,
And could I please get some liniment for the pain in my joints?
The man behind the counter said. Right away you poor thing.
Then he looked at me as if to say, now don't you feel ashamed.
It might sound crazy but I did, feel a little ashamed,
Yet flying above that were the feelings of regret,
For I have not seen the cross over from this stationary time zone.
So I waited, though now with a limited amount of patience.
For my 20 minutes was fast depleting,
And my assurance to be on time for work was quickly fleeting.
But like a nincompoop I allowed my addiction to ground me.
And once more the man behind the counter said,
To number three, with a certainty was not me.
How can I be of assistance?

Now you would have thought but maybe not,
With her witnessing a for sure case of disrespect more than twice,
That she would have done everything within her power to be nice,
But in the case of inferiority, it plays second fiddle to superiority.
Therefore lady three request from the man behind the counter,
Assistance with an item on the same side of the room as she,
Some bottled incense, because she could not decide on a fragrance.
Of course that was right up his alley.
So it became very obvious, that none of them cared about my needs.
And when that door opened once more,
And two others entered,
I recalled what my brother had said about their interior wrappings.
I knew then it was time to go,
For the urgings of Cola was making me old grow.
So I snatched my two dollars that I had laid on his counter,
Then I ran out the door with a great deal of frustration for the bus.
But as I was running to the next block towards the bus stop,
I heard this voice yelling stop thief.
When I turned to look it was the security officer from the corner store.
Well I had no business with that man,
Surely he could not be yelling at me.

# TAGMEWRITE

So I continued running,
But for some strange reason I started to get extremely tired,
My legs felt weak and my heart felt like it was about to stop.
I'm a young person could I be experiencing withdrawal from the lack of Coke?
No that's crazy, that can't be the reason.
Well whatever was going on with this body,
It was slowing me down and no way would I make it to work in this condition,
So I ducked into a nearby alley and decided to address the situation.
But those weak knees of mines gave out and I fell, landing flat on face.
I managed to drag my body behind a trash dumpster,
Then I covered up with this white sheet that someone had tossed away.
I figured that along with the trash dumpster would hide me from security,
Just in case it was me that he was pursuing,
Even though I know I did nothing wrong.

I must have blacked out,
Because when I took a peek from under that white sheet,
The dumpster had been moved and I never heard them move it.
And I was now lying on my left side facing two strangers who looked like paramedics.
I recognized their uniforms because the guys that came to take my brother away,
They were wearing the same identical blue and white attire.
I asked them how they knew where to find me?
The one kneeling beside me said. We received a 911 call that someone was in distress.
The caller was a Female, who chose to remain anonymous,
But she gave us a complete description and location.
He then said. Now I want you to lie completely still because your situation is critical,
And we are afraid that if we move you that it could kill you.
I said. Kill me what in the world is going on? I promise to never drink another coke.
He smiled and looked beyond me.
I said who are you looking at?
Is that security guy behind me?
He said. Yes but how did you know?
I said because I can feel him.
That is when I requested that they completely remove from my body the white sheet,

May 3, 2013    **Jeana Marie Jeffers**

Then tried to roll over to take a good look at the man behind the newspaper,
But the security man was preventing me from rolling on my backside,
He was applying steady pressure to the center of my back.

I demanded an explanation as to why he was touching me.
He said. For the past 15 minutes I've been trying to stop the bleeding.
I said. Stop the bleeding, why am I bleeding?
He said. Because you have a bullet lodged in your back.
Then it got real crazy.
I said. Who shot me?
Then there was total silence.
Security then said it was me.
 I yelled for you to stop but you kept right on running.
I said. So you were yelling at me, but why I hadn't done anything wrong?
He said because it's my job to stop a thief.
And right then I lost it.
Thief! Thief!
Why I've never stole anything in my entire life.
He said I'm not going waste my breathe arguing that point with you little lady,
So as it has already been stated,
You need to calm down and lie still.
All this excitement is only aggravating your condition.
 And what I'm trying to do right now is offer you a helping hand.
Then I said. So now you want to help me.
What's the problem your conscience bothering you?
The security guy replied. No my conscience is fine.
Bottom line,
If it comes down to choosing between YOU,
And keeping a roof over the head of my family,
Well if business is slow, then I call out a thief.
But if you persistently say that there is no thief,
Then that puts my job on the line,
Therefore one of us has got to go.
And it surely is not going to be me.

Internal thought.
You have got to be kidding. I must be having a nightmare.
I then responded. But you shot me in the back,
And you don't find anything wrong with that?
Security Man then states. No I was aiming for your leg,
But then you tripped and stumbled.

# TAGMEWRITE

And that's the story that I explained to the officer over there,
Along with these two paramedics here trying help save your life.
Save my life. You missed that opportunity back at the corner store,
When you sat by and did nothing,
From the moment I walked through the door.
No! You thought that Owners disrespectful behavior was funny,
And just sat there reading that stupid newspaper as if all was good.
And then like a fool you accuse me of stealing,
Chase after me for nothing and then shoot me.
Take your hands off me I'm probably better off dead.
The only mistake I made was not listening to my brothers warning,
And for that I will never be able to enjoy the taste of Cola again.
What I don't understand is the fact that you are a black man,
How can you stand by and not get involved for a righteous cause?
He said I did when I came after you for stealing that money on the counter.
And I did the exact same thing two months ago on the night your brother died.
And his last dying words were the same as yours,
I didn't do it!

*Author / Jeana Marie Jeffers*

**TAG ME**
**INSOMNIA**

Around the entire globe people suffer from me,
As we sit up all night eating popcorn and watching TV.

And it was I, pacing the floor with the spouse of Queen Esther all night.
And if Nebuchadnezzar had no dream, he would not have given me light.

The Doctors and shrinks say I exist because of consistently poor habits.
But if that were the source then why do they treat all of YOU just like lab rabbits?

Oh Well!
Whatever the cause I'm glad the Redacteur stayed awake to include my story,
Since I see no reason why,
Yawn,
You're just about finished lady,
Now complete that last rhyme.
Why ALL those other TAGS should receive ALL the glory.

May 3, 2013  **Jeana Marie Jeffers**

*Author / Jeana Marie Jeffers*

**TAG ME**
**KILLER WHALE**

Hey Bubbles what you doing?
Well I'm pretending to try and master a new trick.
Why do you have to pretend?
Because if you haven't figured it out already Dolly,
There is a connection between performance and reward.
And these humans think that they are teaching us new tricks.
When in reality it is we who are training them to do our bidding.
You see rolling in the water is something delightful to them.
But it was my ancestors from long ago to discover spiral swimming.
It's just something that we do, but these people think it's something new.
So last week when they gave me a demonstration,
I did everything within my power to keep from laughing.
I attentively watched my trainer as if I knew nothing,
Then I gave her this puzzled look as if her instructions were unclear.
Though I was only waiting for her incentive to appear.
 And there it was tasty morsels for my palate.
So, I gave in to the command of a roll, and then I rolled for her again.
I was trying to win her heart, of which that I most certainly did.
And now she wants me to jump through hoops,
I guess she doesn't realize that I'm a breaching expert,
Although that is a good thing because I don't want her feelings hurt.
So I'm going to practice a little more then I'm going to get my reward.
I do say that this is the good life,
I don't have to hunt or sneak up on my supper anymore,
All I have to do is satisfy my employer.
Oh and I'll be shooting my very first video this week.
Along with cutting a brand new CD set to MP3.
They seem to be very intrigued by my resonating sound.
Who knows I might like some of my other cousins,
Land a movie career.
Dolly then said.
Watch out now!
Soon they might have to deflate your ego.

*Author / Jeana Marie Jeffers*

# TAGMEWRITE

*Author / Jeana Marie Jeffers*

**TAG ME**
**KIMONO**

I'm a cultural belle of silk in my country.
My tapestry painted like Irises by Van Gogh.
I'm very courteous with my humbling walk.
And I speak of harmony though I do not talk.

*Author / Jeana Marie Jeffers*

**TAG ME**
**LADY CARDINAL**

Oh Kachoo you are such a romantic,
Breathing all down my neck,
That fresh scent of sunflower fragrance,
I know you've come to make your proposal,
But I would like to get better acquainted,
Then maybe I will accept your seeded gifts.
And even though you're looking mighty fly,
In that red-breasted suit,
I'm a lady and desire to be courted properly,
Though I'm thankful that your gift wasn't slimy,
Seeing me gag on a rope is not very lady-like,
Ok! Go ahead and do your thing.  Woo Me.

*Author / Jeana Marie Jeffers*

**TAG ME**
**LANGUAGE**

The sound of a penguin when courting his mate is a hoot.
When his newly-wed returns about 65 days later they sing.
We imitate the animal gestures by silent finger motions.
Some wag their tails, twitch their ears or flap their wings.
Don't forget the wolf high upon a cliff howling at the moon.
Who is she calling or is this some type of special warning?
There's the greeting of our giant floppy eared elephants.
They say lay it on me baby and give me that warm snot.
Wow, what a nice expression of love.

## May 3, 2013 — Jeana Marie Jeffers

And then there is US.
The HUMAN
When you use me, you either build up or tear down.
And often we choose the latter.
You use me with your facial expressions, body gestures, etc.
And best of all you use me in over 400 different dialects.
Now that is something pretty about me.

*Author / Jeana Marie Jeffers*

**TAG ME**
**LIFE PRESERVERS**

We're ALL in training and want to be good at what we do.
Roll call.
Jackets and Vest – READY
Boats and Dinghies – READY
Doctors, EMT'S, Firemen, Officers – READY
Divers – READY
Centurions – READY
The Elderly – READY

Umm – Excuse me sir.
But how does that last call fit in our training exercise?
Haven't you ever heard Soldier the old saying take a lesson from the wise?
MAKE A DIFFERENCE.

*Author / Jeana Marie Jeffers*

**TAG ME**
**LIGHT**

I was part of the pronouncements, it was good.
And temporarily separated from my Brother,
But it was only by a daily division of twelve.

Unlike him, I do not suffer from low self esteem.
For I always keep my lantern set on high beam.
But it was Brother who made my world so bright.
He said to me with his deep dark voice.
I will be one thing and you can be the other,

# TAGMEWRITE

So I chose to be the one our Father would call Day.

*Author / Jeana Marie Jeffers*

**TAG ME**
**LION**

Huff, Huff, Huff, Huff,
Whew, something is definitely wrong with this picture.
Why are those stalkers chasing after me?
Is it because they crowned me king of the jungle?

Huff, Huff, Huff, Huff,
Hey what is that over there?
It looks like a temple.
Maybe I can find somewhere to hide.
But quick I know those stalkers can't be too far behind.

Huff, Huff, Huff, Huff
Oh great there are two more of me at the top of the stairs.
Hey you two I would not stay out here in the open like this,
Because there are 10 men and 10 women headed this direction,
And they all are carrying rifles and I think they want to celebrate.

Hey!
Did you hear what I just said?
We need to go find a good place to hide.
Look partner,
(SLAPPING THE IDOL ON THE BACK)
Oh no!
(NOW RUBBING THE IDOL SURFACE)
Aaaaaaaaaaaaaaaaa!
What have they done to you?
They have turned you both into golden statues.
I think I'll go inside and take a quick tour of this shrine circus.
Oh no!
This place is worse than I thought.
Everywhere I turn,
They have imprisoned some poor creature in a shell skin made of rock.
I can't stay here!
There is nothing but still life here.
This must be what is really meant by Animal Kingdom.

So now who's going to worship the ground I walk on?
Yoo-hoo stalkers I'm in here.

*Author / Jeana Marie Jeffers*

## TAG ME
## MARGE SIMPSON

I represent the conscience of families everywhere.
And my creator made me animated with big blue hair.
Of which I choose to say is a representation of the sea,
But like it you really don't want to ever aggravate me.

My green dress was designed to cover the world over.
We therefore root our trees for generations to handover.
Though I do not understand the beads and shoes of red,
But I'm guessing they symbolize the ground is being feed.

Oh how I do try very hard to keep my family in line.
Let me see you keep it together with miracle like minds.
It can only be a dream to wish for one big happy family.
But just do your best and remember to turn OFF that TV.

*Author / Jeana Marie Jeffers*

## TAG ME
## MARRIED

I'm so glad that I waited for this moment.
Even though all is not perfect,
If I had ran ahead of my indecisive heart,
Perfection would be the portrait wanted.

But how did I outgrow my unrealistic fantasies?
I had to sit down and take a good look at myself,
Then decide if I could be good to someone else.
Though I could only fill my head with future lies.

So for years I processed all of my expectations,
Then I learned on site a few to do's or not to do's.
Then I put them all together and prayed for help.

# TAGMEWRITE

And then I was able to move on, to a better song.

*Author / Jeana Marie Jeffers*

**TAG ME**
**MERCEDES BENZ**

They finally made the perfect model for me.
And they graded you A, high honors indeed.
All you needed to pass by me was 100 percent.
But you went and doubled the score, EXCELLENT!

I see not obsolete in your future or saying farewell.
Since your birth you have shaped an amazing trail.
One that prevented me from cheating on you,
Neither did I have a longing to be driven by another.

So as I'm perching in the comfort of your leather.
I smile at me in your mirror for having it together.
Then I think. What if I'm becoming a lover of Material?
Then back to Germany you'll go, and I'll keep Spiritual.

*Author / Jeana Marie Jeffers*

**TAG ME**
**MIRAGE**

I tried touching my face in the watered reflection but I disappeared.
It must have been a contrast of heaven that made me look in there.

Wilting from the swallowed sand my perspiration caused to evolve.
I see rising above the sun, giant bees, palm trees and even Taj Mahal.

I finally reach a nice cool place to spread the news of feathered glory.
But same as Gideon's Angel had vanished so did the end of this story.

*Author / Jeana Marie Jeffers*

**TAG ME**
**MIRROR**

Your outlook on life is distorted.

May 3, 2013  **Jeana Marie Jeffers**

I know this because I see something different.

Mary, you see a woman filled with sadness.
What I see is a sheep that will help turn the world around.

Peter you see yourself as a stud with the strength of Hercules.
What I see is a man in need of a reality check. But there's hope.

Vashti you see a lady with the entire world rotating around you.
What I see is vanity, needing to change her ways or get dumped.

David you see yourself as a man unworthy of forgiveness.
What I see is a great leader who will stand by his fellowman.

So EVERYONE, check YOURSELVES out daily.
That way you won't come to me being something you are not.

*Author / Jeana Marie Jeffers*

**TAG ME**
**MISTAKE**

*This story is not about insults.*
*It is just a story to make YOU think.*

As soon as I turned eighteen I was out of the house.
That was the moment I had waited for my entire life.
Always taking orders and following parental rules.
Feeling hopelessly lost and totally misunderstood.

But I knew that if ever that day would come,
I would walk out that door and I would never look back.
And that is exactly what I did, now time to share the facts.

I know you're wondering how an eighteen year old survived.
You will have to read to the end because it's possible I died.

Though I was a city girl the place that I grew up was slow pace.
But I had always dreamed of one day moving to the Big Apple.
So that is where I ran to live out my fantasies, at a much faster pace.

# TAGMEWRITE

Again how would I survive, moving way out there?
Well, I had taken up a trade in High School.
Then I went online to search for a position in that field.
But it had to fit my needs, which was location, location, location.
And Voila!
There it was an opening in my field and located in New York City.

I was confident that I would have no problem landing the position.
And why not, I'm talented and believe that dreams do come true.
And since every single thing was falling perfectly in place,
I knew that my time had arrived so I did not hesitate.

I packed only what I needed and that wasn't very much.
Then I embraced the photo of my parents and said, Goodbye.
It had to be that way because any other path would have been prevented.

I arrived in New York on a Thursday morning.
That was the longest bus trip that I had ever taken and I was exhausted.
So, I was very much in need of a shower and a nice soft bed.
I walked up to the window clerk and asked for directions.
I handed him a piece of paper with an address.
The address was where this twenty two year old named Von resided.
Von had moved away from my hometown to Queens about 3 years ago.
And we decided to keep in touch.
She had a small apartment in Queens,
And she had invited me to come and stay with her until I got on my feet.

To survive Von worked as a stripper.
But I don't judge, in fact I totally agree with the saying,
 TO EACH HIS OWN!
The point is we were as different as night and day.
I was shy, not much of a socialite but I was curious.
Von was a party girl, loved to entertain and adventurous.
Hence, I knew it wouldn't be long, before I would move on.

After about 4 months that is exactly what I did.
I could no longer put up with all of her late night guests.
And many mornings waking up to find the apartment a total mess.
Therefore, to maintain our friendship I moved.

I wasn't making enough money on an entry level journalist salary.
So I had to move to a place that would be within my budget.

## May 3, 2013 — Jeana Marie Jeffers

I moved in a house with many rooms for rent.
This time I had to share both bathroom and kitchen with 4 other occupants.
The bathroom situation was somewhat a problem,
But I pretty much ate in my bedroom.
My bedroom, I loved the sound of that.
Behind those four walls I felt right at home.
Unlike before, I shared that space with no one.

No more having to sleep on the hideaway bed,
That I shared with 2 miniature felines.
I guess because I was home more so than Von,
They just became attached.

And no more sleeping in Von's bed,
Whenever she wanted to confiscate mines, or hers,
So that she could party or get busy.

But that is the past and I'm now moving forward.

So in my little four cornered room is where I lived for the next 3 years.
Not being able to afford to move, for as of yet,
I had not received a substantial pay increase.
And because of those late night classes,
That I was taking to try and excel in my professional journalist field,
I had to keep a very low spending profile.
But it wouldn't be long before the rest of my dream would come to life.

There was a story that I very much wanted to cover.
It centered around a serial killer that every 1st Tuesday of the month,
He would strangle a female victim inside their homes.
Then he would leave them propped up at the dining table,
With a pink silk scarf tied around their neck.
He became known as the 1st Tuesday Strangler.

The strangler had been apprehended.
That is how we knew of his gender.
And my boss who was just as curious as I, wanted to know,
What his motives were for the killings?

Why the pink scarf?

# TAGMEWRITE

Why he left them sitting up straight at the dining table?
And why the 1st Tuesday was so significant?

I personally wanted to know how he gained access.
Especially since the women were warned,
To stay off the streets after a certain hour if possible,
Or at least if WE had too, not to go out alone,
And not open our doors to any unknown strangers.

None of them had anything in common
So did he know his victims?

Well if I was ever going to make it in this business,
Then I needed a break so that I could prove myself capable.
That would mean I would have to come from behind the desk,
And step out there in the world to investigate.
Loving It!

So out of the blue, my boss Mr. Staples placed me in charge.
Well it wasn't so much out of the blue.

I woke up on the wrong side of the bed and decided to throw a tantrum.
That was one of the items packed in my suitcase when I moved to New York.

It was time to upload my confidence.
So, in the privacy of Mr. Staple's office,
I merely brought to his attention that I had something more to offer,
Than just sitting behind a desk and cleaning up everyone's mess.
And that I was starting to feel used.
If he truly liked my journalism skills,
Then he was going to have to consider opening up for me another door.

Now!
Out of the blue,
He said you're right!
I have an interview scheduled today at 11:00,
And it just so happens that our strangler,
Has a special request.
He will only share his story with someone new.
So I'm placing you in charge of this cover story.
I trust you to get the facts,
And I know Currie that you won't let me down.

## May 3, 2013 — Jeana Marie Jeffers

I was flabbergasted.
Isn't that something, you can be confident and surprised at the same time.

Well off I went to gather all the facts.
The man behind bars had only agreed to interview with me.
That must be a sign.

The interview was very startling.
Some things he said, though bizarre,
Just did not fall completely into place.
But because this was my golden opportunity,
I made the puzzle pieces come together as if working towards a Pulitzer.

While I was typing those win me a complete place of my own words,
I could feel the changes in the air,
And hear the sweet sound of success tickling my ears.

Yes that article did as I suspected.
It opened up many more doors.
I was now on the road to success.

Mr. Staples allowed me to cover many more stories.
I proved to be an honest, hard working competitor.
So, he placed me second in command in case of his absence.
And he also gave me a handsome raise up front in profit.

I'm living the dream,
Now just 21 and doing my own thing.

I decided to celebrate by going on a shopping spree.
I moved on up like the Jefferson's, and purchased a condo with a balcony.
And guess where?
You know it! New York City baby!
I picked out some furniture some new clothes, shoes, changed my hair,
Started wearing make-up, pedicure, manicure, you know, the works.

I started eating stuff like caviar,
Drinking the good stuff like Bordeaux.
But there was one problem,
After 5 months of fame,

# TAGMEWRITE

I realized that I hadn't made any real friends.
It was time to step out of my shell and let someone in.

But the problem was where?
I didn't want to be picked up by someone at a bar.
That sounded cheesy.
Besides I wasn't looking for a one night stand.
I was looking for someone to call friend.

So just like everything else that has taken place in my life,
Came together at the right time, I decided to let
That part of my dream, to be loved schedule itself too.

And wouldn't you know it, right on time,
I met a guy at the corner market,
Two weeks after I buried the thought.

He was the perfect gentleman.
He treated all women with respect.
And no he wasn't a flirt, he just was packaged right.
He was smart, funny and never put on any airs.

The first time we met,
He said that he had been watching me for some time,
But with everything going on in the news,
With the 1st Tuesday Strangler, he was afraid that
With him being a stranger that he would spook me.
Therefore, he was waiting for the right moment to approach me.

I said watching me, watching me from where?
And if you've seen me why haven't I seen you?
He said. Though I live around here,
Every Tuesday I ride the subway into Queens to visit my father.
After spending most of the day with him,
I would head back and see you getting off the train.
The first time I noticed you was when this elderly man stumbled,
And you reached out quickly and caught him before he fell.
But you didn't stop there, you went the distance,
And grabbed his hand, then you walked him to safety.
Every since then I could not stop thinking about you.
I saw something good in you and wanted to get to know you.
So when Tuesday rolled back around,

### May 3, 2013 — Jeana Marie Jeffers

Not only did I enjoy spending time with my father,
But, now I looked forward to seeing your face every Tuesday.

I was very impressed with him.
In my opinion this was the beginning to a perfect friendship.

For the next two months we exchanged intimate secrets about each other.
Being that he worked out of his home,
Much of our time together was spent at his place.
Then one of his Tuesday visits he taken me to meet his Father.

It was perfect. Because as a token of his appreciation,
Mr. Staples arranged for me to have the day off.

Marco's father, a very nice man, was confined to a bed.
But what I did not know until the day I met his dad,
Was that Marco's mom was alive because he never spoke of her.

At the time of the visit she was there.
She was very pleasant and they seemed to get along well.
So I inquired later as to why he never mentioned to me about his mom.

He said, well we don't always see eye to eye when it comes to Dad.
I'm sure that she wants the best for him,
But I would like for her to respect how I feel about him too.
But that is never going to happen,
Even before Dad ended up in the condition he is now,
She has never taken me serious or even understood me.

I can relate to that.

He said, with all that you have told me,
That I can believe.

I tell you what, enough of this talk about mother.
She will be leaving town this weekend, with a friend of hers.
So I'm going to give her a break and stay with Dad,
Until she returns home on Tuesday morning.

So how about we have dinner at your place,
And I'm going to provide the meal,

# TAGMEWRITE

And do all the cooking.

I responded. Sounds like a perfect evening to me.

We are making headway now.
I've been to his place.
I've met both his parents.
And now he is stepping over into my world.
Yeah!

Well now it is Tuesday,
And the entire day all I could think about was tonight.
This was going to be the news story to make headlines,
"I Found A Friend."

Since everything had been wrapped up early for the day,
And Mr. Staples was out of town on business.
I decided to leave someone else in charge and go home.

I arrived home about 4pm and quickly took a shower,
And changed into something more comfortable but sexy.

Dinner was scheduled for six.
But I wanted to make sure that the atmosphere was right.
So I selected the music and made sure that my scent was everywhere.

Marco arrived right on time.
He rang my buzzer and I cautiously inquired as to who was calling.
He responded back with, it's me!

I laughed behind the buzzer not wanting to risk insulting him.
Then I buzzed him in.

When I opened the door,
There he stood with a very large but lovely basket and a smile.

I then invited him in and closed the door behind him.
Then said hello, and he said, "Hi", then kissed my lips.
I then said ooh whatever you have in that basket smells delicious.
That is when he started naming off the menu.

He said, I know it has been a long time,

May 3, 2013   **Jeana Marie Jeffers**

Since you've had a real home cooked meal.
So I have fresh greens out of my garden,
Homemade mashed potatoes,
Just the way you like them with lumps.
A beef roast smothered in gravy and onions,
And some home style hot watered corn bread.
Then of course, I brought with me some red wine.
"We will talk dessert later."

I laughed at his flirtatious manners.

By the way he said.
"You look good in that pink off the shoulder lace handkerchief dress.
I like that color on women."

"Thank you baby, you look good to me too in all that black.
Now let's eat I'm starving."

The meal was fantastic.
We sat there eating, talking,
Laughing, and enjoying one another's company.
When dinner was over, together we washed and dried the dishes,
Then we sit down on the sofa with another glass of wine to talk.
By that time, I really wasn't too excited about talking,
I was concentrating on getting to the next stages of sealing our friendship.
But out of appreciation I listened.

I had loaded the mp3 player with a variety of music.
At that particular moment Boney James version of Stop,
Look, Listen to your heart, was playing.

Marco was telling me a story about his Mother that rung strange.
He said. Mother is the cause of Father being bed ridden.
She does not think I know about it,
Because dear old Mom, has been living in total darkness for a very long time.
But I think she is slowly coming around.
You see I had to do something to get her attention.

What are you saying Marco?

Don't you know?

# TAGMEWRITE

It was you who did the interview.
I know that whatever that impostor told you,
Could not have had any ring of truth.
But yet you chose to print a lie and let that man rot in jail,
For crimes that you know within your soul that he did not commit.
Why? Self Interest, that's why.

I stood up and said.
Marco you're scaring me.
I think you better leave now.

Then Marco said. Sit Down!
And if you try to scream for help,
I will go off the grid and cut your throat.

He continues.
My Father worked as a Public Accountant,
And had spent most of his time traveling,
But he was getting older,
I had gone away to college,
Therefore he decided that he needed to spend more time with Mom.
So he cut his schedule down to only traveling 1 week out of the month.

That is when Mother every 1st Tuesday of the month for the past 6 years
After Dad left for his business trips, started having her week long affairs.
It could have started way before then,
But Dad did not start getting suspicious until about a year and a half ago.
That is when the pink silk scarf showed up.
Dad recognized the manufacturer.
It was made and designed in Paris France.
So he knew that she had either been to France without his knowledge,
Or someone else gave her the scarf,
And because of the cost he was sure it was a man.
Not that another woman would not spend that much for a gift,
But Mother was very secretive about the scarf and treasured it.

So to prove his theory,
Dad had scheduled his trip for the second week of the month,
But he never mentioned to Mom about the change.
He wanted to catch her in the act.

Soon as he left for the pretend trip,

**May 3, 2013** — **Jeana Marie Jeffers**

Mom was out the door and headed for Long Island.
Dad followed her to a man named Stanley Staples house.

What! Mr. Staples!
But he is married.

True, but as they say when the cat's away the mice will play.
My Mom and Staples have been lovers for a very long time.

Wait he is out of town now and due back tomorrow.
Your Mother came back today.

Now you're catching on.
The affair stopped after the first three deaths.
They were both convinced that the strangler was me.
But then you ruined that.
And then about 2 months ago,
The affair started again.

That was when you met me.

Bingo!
Well since you never asked,
Allow me to tell you what happened to Dad.

My Father waited all night for Mom to come out,
But that never happened.
He wanted to go up to the door and knock,
But once the lights went out,
All he could do was sit there and cry.
So he drove off in his emotional state of mind, and drove his car off a cliff.

What you see now is the results.
When I came home from school,
Dad told me everything.
So I did some investigating of my own.
And that is how I found out the truth about my dear old Mother.
So her punishment is to take care of Dad for the rest of his or her life.
And now she has to live with the guilt of having a serial killer for a son.
*Marco puts on his gloves at the time of making that statement.*

# TAGMEWRITE

"So you killed those women to punish your Mother?
But how could you condemn them to death for what she did?"

They were all tested just like you!
When I took them, same as I did you, to meet Dad,
Just the same as you, they never inquired about his condition.
But, what they were curious about, and you as well,
Was why I never mentioned to them about my Mother?

Go figure!
There lies a Man in a pitiful state,
But your concern and theirs too, is my disloyal Mother.

"But we had no idea."

"As to whether or not you knew is not the point.
You knew enough to inquire, so why not about him?"

So are you saying that if they had asked about your Dad,
That they might still be alive today?

I won't know the answer to that question until it happens.
But the way I see it every last one of you are just like Mom,
SELFISH!

That's not true in my case.
Remember the old man that you saw me helping.
Don't that count for something?

Currie baby, please.
You just wrote a story that condemned an innocent man to death.
So you helped that old man to ease your own conscience.
Because of guilt, that is why Mom is helping Dad.
But she hasn't learned anything about loyalty.

What makes you any better than us Marco,
You lied to me and no doubt all the others,
Just so you could avenge your Father.

That's where you are wrong.
I never once lied to any of you.
See you're confusing not telling you everything with a lie.

## May 3, 2013 — Jeana Marie Jeffers

Don't that sound strange to you?
Don't answer that.
All of a sudden you're an expert on lies.
You adjust how you view things according to your situation.
The man lying on death row meant a profit.
Then the man standing before you right now,
You accuse of lying with false reasoning,
But in reality you're trying to bargain with me for your life.
That's SAD.

You poor thing you started off wrong from the beginning.
You bring nothing but pain to every life that you touch.
Unlike me, you had a very good Mother,
But you turned your back on her,
And never ever wrote her a letter to let her know you were OK.
That is a major failure on your part, and that is going to cost you.
And today is the 1st Tuesday of the month.
But you consider yourself privileged.
Because you are the only one that I ever told the whole truth,
And you're going to carry it with you to your grave sweet baby.
And dear old Mom is going to know for sure that she created a monster.

I was now facing the dragon and I wanted my Mommy.
I wanted to tell her that I was sorry for hurting her and Daddy.
Marco, please, no.
You said you loved me.

And I do my darling.
But I love my Father too.
And my first place loyalty belongs to him.

I try to run for the door and I scream.
But Marco places his hand over my mouth and drags me to the dining room table.
I try hard to fight back, but he over powers me.
Then he reaches inside the basket and pulls out a pink silk scarf.
Then he slowly and firmly pulls the scarf tight,
And then strangles the life out of Mademoiselle Currie.

He then props her up in the chair at the table,
Combs her hair and wipes away her tears,

# TAGMEWRITE

Kisses her goodbye, then exits apartment 607 with his basket.
*The exit song on the mp3 is Lalah Hathaway's "Breathe."*

But as he is walking down the hallway,
The lady in apartment 610 opens her door and say,
Excuse me sir.
Did you hear someone scream?

No ma'am I'm sorry I did not.
Maybe you heard a scream on the TV down the hall.
Or could it be your mind playing tricks on you?

No I'm sure the scream I heard was real.

Marco said as he slowly approached her.
It's possible.
But I think you made a _____.
DOOR CLOSING
Locks CLICK, CLICK, CLICK

*Author / Jeana Marie Jeffers*

## TAG ME
## MODERATION

They only asked for forty,
But I said I'll give you fifty.
Then the voice within me said,
That's too much!

They wanted a little recreation,
But I said I want a lot.
Then the voice within me said,
That's too much!

They offered me a healthy diet,
But I said I'm use to grease.
Then the voice within me said,
That's too much

They told me to drink more water,
But I said no we need more booze.

Then the voice within me said,
That's too much!

They labeled me an extremist.
I said you are absolutely right.
Then the voice within me said,
That is what you might be,
But I'm just the opposite.

*Author / Jeana Marie Jeffers*

**TAG ME**
**MUHAMMAD ALI**

I was formed out of clay,
And was shaped into a legend,
And though I did not eat much humble pie,
My strong convictions turned out pleasant.

I've been idolized and VILIFIED,
During the course of my glorious years,
But I stayed ready, and kept to the count,
And spoke poetic trash in defense of my career.

I am the Greatest.
You are the Greatest.
Yes he is the Greatest.
And now it is unanimous.

*Author / Jeana Marie Jeffers*

**TAG ME**
**MUSIC**

Wow where do I begin.
You know that you asked me a two part question.
How did I get started in this business?
So I'm going to start by separating the two.
I am not a business or industry,
Those are labels that the money makers invented.
And they came on the scene way, way after me.

# TAGMEWRITE

In fact, my existence started with the very first syllables.
He spoke something meaningful,
And wrote them down on a note pad,
Then magically what he spoke came to life.
And there I was dancing across the broadways.

You see,
I also work in conjunction with a mood.
It can be a good mood or a bad mood.
A happy mood or a sad mood,
Insane or sane,
Affectionate or moody,
I don't question it.
I just perform it.
I give it harmony,
Connect the thoughts with the results,
And then I am placed on a rhythmic scale.
Though your imagination is what sets the tone.

That's beautiful.
Thank You

*Author / Jeana Marie Jeffers*

**TAG ME**
**PARADISE**

While skipping through this lovely garden,
I was overcome with this fixation for longevity,
For everywhere I looked was a blessed miracle,
That dripped oil across my skin with beauty.

I climbed beautiful mountains without fear,
And played with animals from every kingdom,
I took a dip in the ocean no longer polluted,
Then I stroked the flipper of the humpbacked whale.

Now tell me on what forbidden Island have I crashed,
Where everywhere I turn peace is the trumpet blast,
And where no self indulgence can rob me of prosperity?
It must be the park of imagination where real is fantasy.

May 3, 2013  **Jeana Marie Jeffers**

*Author / Jeana Marie Jeffers*

**TAG ME**
**PATIENCE**

You know it is taking forever for that dough to rise.
Just wait it will happen.
Boy I sure wish that the summer would hurry and come.
Just wait it will happen.
How many hours left before the sun comes up?
Just wait it will happen.
You know it has taken forever for there to be a black President.
Just wait it will happen.
You know I don't believe that Armageddon is ever coming.
Just wait it will happen.
You know if you would daily apply a tiny bit of me,
You would be surprised at how much easier waiting could be.

*Author / Jeana Marie Jeffers*

**TAG ME**
**PIANO**

Well I'm glad that's over.
So now I guess it's my turn to speak.

I have not a prejudice bone in my body,
Being that my bi-racial family are black and white.
Coming from a long line of poetic musicians,
I'm able to synthesize my harmony day and night.

I'm strikingly talented and do love traveling abroad,
Being accompanied by the versatile woodwind family,
And the powerful sound of our best friend the amazing brass.
Smile Frenchie and Obie.
Then we have the percussions that do me competitive justice.
Play on Glockie.
YOU Bad Mamma Jamma YOU!
And last but not least we have multiple strings.
Just look at how polished she looks.
When she plays, every single stroke comes out clean.

# TAGMEWRITE

Take your bow Violie.

So just like our mentor, I'm proud of them too.
The audience claps and anticipates our every whistle.
They keep me on my toes for when it's time to blend in.

ALL TOGETHER – We love you too! Solo.
Frenchie – Especially after you deliver your keynote address.

Mentor – Don't slight yourself Solo, I'm proud of you also.
Interviewer – wiping tears.  Me too,
Now!
How about you joining the rest of them,
And give us a little performance.
Solo – Sounds good to me.
Frenchie – Let's get ready.  It's time to make love.
Violie – Let it go Obie.

*Author / Jeana Marie Jeffers*

**TAG ME
RESPECT**

I make it all about YOU.
That is what Momma said to do.
She did not say it because she was humble.
But because she did not want to see ANYONE stumble.

Momma said to smile is a blessing from above.
So that is my gift to YOU and I give it with love.
If WE do our best to follow the fine example set by Mother.
Then WE can willingly accept that WE are BLOOD Brothers.

So now I'm going to introduce to YOU,
The woman responsible for my existence,
I now humbly, lovingly, and willingly give YOU my Mom.
THE GOLDEN RULE!

*Author / Jeana Marie Jeffers*

## Jeana Marie Jeffers
May 3, 2013

**TAG ME**
**ROSES**

I want to shower your hair in the sweet scent of Apricot.
I want to feel at home with you,
So you can shine like Crimson in the window.
I want to petal my Lavender straight to your soft bath water.
I want to lay bare on your white Linen and watch you fall asleep.
I want to dip you like Orange sherbet as we dance the night away.
I want to taste your Peach body sugar,
As I run my tongue across your shoulders.
I want to kiss your shaded Pink lips until the moon is no more.
I want to place upon your Russet finger,
That love knot that will forever tie us together.
I want to seal our bloodline with Scarlet,
Because I screened our DNA and we're compatible.
I wanted to be sure to include Yellow,
Because I knew this one was your favorite.

These are the romantic words that the real Man in your life will utter,
Right after he personally hands you one by one, all ten forgive me's.
Then of course you say, but not in that exact order right. (SMILE)

*Author / Jeana Marie Jeffers*

**TAG ME**
**SCANDALOUS**

Ok this is going to blow your mind.
It's a story about a man in a motorized wheel chair,
And we're going to call him Willie.
Well one day Willie was out visiting a few friends.
He made his first stop at the corner barber shop.
The barber shop was always a place of comfort.
Willie could tell a few jokes and laugh a little.
After about an hour or so, Willie said his goodbyes,
And out the door he rolled in the direction of the market.
He had about $15 in his pocket and wanted to buy,
Bread, Hotdogs, and a small package of ground beef.
Those were the items that he had written down.

# TAGMEWRITE

He loved chili dogs and was going to have them for supper.
He was a thrifty shopper and knew the bread would cost
About a $1, the hotdogs about $2 because they were
Made with turkey, and the ground beef about $1 for
It was a markdown item because of the expiration date.
So $4 was all he expected to spend on his dinner.
Then after paying exactly what he had calculated,
Willie rolled on down the street to the drug store.
He needed to pick up two prescriptions.
One was for the pain in his lower back and legs,
The other was for his blood pressure.
The cost for both prescriptions was a co-pay of $4 each.
So now he is left with only $3 and Willie like most of us,
Who loves kicking back to an ice cold Beer,
Asked the lady behind the checkout counter,
To ring him up a 40 ounce of Old English.
After paying for that he was now left with a $1.
Before leaving Willie told her a joke.
Why?
Because that was something she had grown accustomed to.
Then he rolled away laughing with his Bread, Hotdogs,
His Ground Beef, Med's and a 40.
Willie had rolled about two blocks in the direction of town,
Crossed the busy intersection at 36th and Illinois,
Was just about at his apartment on 36th and Meridian,
When this guy jumped out of nowhere,
Pointing a gun in Willie's face and demanding money.
Willie said,
Man I ain't got nothing but a dollar.
The guy said, give it to me.
Willie reached in his pocket and pulled out his last dollar,
Then he handed it over to the armed man.
Then the man said,
What else you got?
Willie said just a meal and something for me to drink.
The armed man took that from Willie too.
Willie said that is all I have left to eat.
What am I suppose to do for food?
The guy said,
What's more important right now, your life or your big belly?
Willie said well naturally I'm going to choose my life.
The guy said, then shut up and hand over that other bag.

May 3, 2013  **Jeana Marie Jeffers**

Willie said man no not that,
I need these for pain and to keep my blood pressure under control.
The man said, I'll tell you what.
I will give you the blood pressure medicine,
Because I'm sure after this you're going to need them.
But I'm keeping the prescription for pain.
I'm sure that I can get something for them off the streets.
But I'm also taking your wheel chair.
My grandmother could use a nice chair like this.
So he takes Willie by the arm and drags him to the ground.
Then he sits in the wheel chair and rolls away,
With the Bread, Hotdogs, Ground Beef, Pain Medicine, 40 and chair.
Now I think I should tell you how Willie ended up in the wheel chair.
One night he was coming home from work and had just got off the bus.
As he was crossing the street,
A car sped around the corner and struck him.
The driver fled the scene leaving Willie for dead.
But as you can see, Willie is a survivor.
So after about 15 minutes had passed by,
Because Willie maintained a perfect record in punctuality,
Two of Willie's friends started to inquire as to Willie's whereabouts.
When no one could give them a satisfactory response,
They took off in search of their dear friend.
It did not take them long at all to find Willie.
Being that Willie had previously informed them where he was headed.
They found Willie around the corner on 36th street.
He was sitting there with his back up against a sycamore tree.
As they approached him, Willie just looked at them and laughed.
He said a funny thing happened to me today.
I got wheelchair jacked.
Both men looked at each other strangely,
Because they knew whatever happened wasn't a laughing matter.
But after about 30 seconds the humor started to sink in.
So they like Willie started laughing their heads off too.
When all three men finally composed themselves,
The two friends stood on opposite sides of Willie,
Then they each placed on arm under Willie's arms,
And their other arm under Willie's legs and carried him home.
Once there one of the friends called to report the incident.
When the police officer arrived,
Willie was grateful that it was someone he knew.

# TAGMEWRITE

Confident that justice would be served.
The officer wrote down every single detail,
Not missing a beat.
Then before he left,
He told Willie not to worry that tonight dinner was on him.
Everyone in the neighborhood knew that Willie was just an ordinary man,
And that he lived on a fixed disability income.
At times to make extra cash he hustled or collected a few beer cans to sale.
So the police officer just did not feel right just leaving and doing nothing.
But out of respect for Willie and all that he had been through,
He dignified Willie by saying,
Which do you prefer, Chinese, fried chicken with potato salad, or chili dogs?
Willie said, Man those first two choices sound real good,
But my heart was set on those chili dogs.
Then chili dogs it is.
Then before the officer closed the door,
Willie jokingly gave the officer a tip.
He said Man I truly respect what you do,
But you keep alert out there because these perpetrators today are
_____.

That night Willie watched basketball with his friends,
They all ate chili dogs and enjoyed an ice cold beer.
And the very next day Willie's wheelchair was returned by the officer.
And the thief was caught red handed selling Willie's prescription on the corner of 38th
Stupid!  But that is not it.

These perpetrators today are _____.

*Author / Jeana Marie Jeffers*

**TAG ME**
**SEQUOIA TREES**

Come, ride the elevator and see what it's like atop of my world.
Just step inside those double doors and push level one zero four.
Now, take a look around, and poetically recite what it is you see.

As I slide in circular motion by way of your connecting skywalk.
I see infinite purple mountains that take me on a mile high ride.
I see beyond the leaves of your bigger than life majestic limbs,
The blinding rays of sun with a proposal for peace to be-wed.

### May 3, 2013 — Jeana Marie Jeffers

I taste and smell fresh air because it is much cleaner than below.
I see stretched for miles a flowered quilt of assorted meadows.
I hear laughter and echoing smiles ringing in every nearby town.
The view up here is so lovely that I don't ever want to come down.

And you don't have too!
You can build your nest up here with us.
Our roots are strong.
We can stand our ground against any quakes.
We don't have problems with flooding.
And we have our own guaranteed 3000 year term life insurance policy.

*Author / Jeana Marie Jeffers*

## TAG ME
## SKELETON BONES

I'm stronger than steel,
Your bare frame sex appeal,
My diploma supports the Anatomy field.
Was used as a prank in the house of thrills,
Surgically removed so she could come alive,
After touching those of Elisha he was revived,
Without me YOU would certainly be deprived.
So get milk, then I can bust a move and survive.
Whew! It's hard being me.
Ha, Ha, Ho, Ho, I made a funny.

*Author / Jeana Marie Jeffers*

## TAG ME
## SLEEP WALKER

In this realm I perform task out of the ordinary.
I wash the dishes, and return to the real world.

Another time I fed the cat, cleaned the toilet,
And then again I returned to the real world.

Next, I painted a red X on all my neighbor's doors.

# TAGMEWRITE

And then again I returned to the real world.

Then this world of strange turned for the worse.
I drove my car down a one way street.
What startled me were the honking horns.
But by the oncoming lights I was not fazed.

Quickly I steer the car into an empty lot.
With my palms all sweaty and my heart racing,
I look around and for the first time realize,
My roommate was reaping all the rewards.

*Author / Jeana Marie Jeffers*

**TAG ME**
 **SNAKE**

The human tongue can be hypocritical,
And if used improperly can send a mixed signal.
Though my tongue as well is two directional,
I do not ignore my tongues guiding principles.

For if I do,
Ignore the prodding's of my fork in the road,
Then when I'm hidden in the bush,
With my radar aimed at you,
And unzipping skin to lighten my load,
Instead of exercising the right,
I would renounce my will to crush,
Instead of loving the hunt,
I would hate the pursuit of warm blooded stew,
All of which would go contrary to nature,
Therefore I would be just as swishy washy as YOU.

*Author / Jeana Marie Jeffers*

**TAG ME**
**SOAP**

My chemical components are plant ashes and seaweed.
I don't swim with the mermaids but lavish with Jacuzzis.
I'm a variety basket of perfumed scents and colorful dyes.

Make you feel like silk while sipping on a glass of Sunrise.

*Author / Jeana Marie Jeffers*

**TAG ME**
**SOMBRERO**

Hey poppy, you sure put a whole new twist to fill it to the brim.
What you doing running around looking like Speedy Gonzalez?
I could ask the same question but you look more like Roy Rogers.
Wait! I don't think you completely understand how to Jone.
You telling me that I look like Roy Rogers that's a real compliment.
Well I guess it is all according to how you hear it. Correct?
You were trying to poke fun at me because of how I look.
And I was poking fun at you because you want to be me and missed.
What I'm wearing is a classic and what you're wearing is an imitation.
My people made this to serve a good purpose and we wear it proud.
I suggest you stop joning and be proud of the vaquero you're wearing.
Happy trails to you.

*Author / Jeana Marie Jeffers*

**TAG ME**
**SPIDER**

I hang out on the corner with my man fearless fly.
But if we don't change our habits he or I could die.
Though he's know to get around faster than me,
One quick tug on my rope, I propel as if I had wings.

I love adventure, so I spy on humans when they read.
Sugar head fearless gets caught, so I go set him free.
I'm not a super hero, but oh how I do love the hype.
But it's time for me to bounce, or my y-fee, will bite.

*Author / Jeana Marie Jeffers*

**TAG ME**
**STARS**

We are about to pull off the greatest heist in all the universe,

# TAGMEWRITE

We are going to steel 5,000 diamonds worth 25,000,000,000,
Straight out of the night deposit box of the Stellar Space Building.
And the best part about this caper is that no one will ever miss them.
You know why?
Because there are billions and billions and billions and billions and,
Ok, we get the point.
They have billions and billions.
Exactly!
They have so many that they can't even keep account of them all.
Ok, so what's the plan?
Ok pay very close attention.
Tomorrow night at midnight,
The four of us are going to board the shuttle,
But to avoid any suspicion,
We will enter one at a time 10 minutes after the other.
We need to bring enough rope to string 1,250 diamonds each.
Rock, you TAG the Ash collection.
Stone, you can TAG the Kesil's.
Jewel, you're assigned to TAG the Kimah's.
And I will be responsible for TAGGING the Mazzaroth collection.
Now once we enter that shuttle and push the start button,
We have exactly five days to complete our mission.
So there is no turning back.
I think you mean there is no coming back.
Count me out.
Me too,
Me also,
What's the matter you afraid of getting burned?

*Author / Jeana Marie Jeffers*

**TAG ME**
**STEEL MAGNOLIAS**

I'm a Hybrid.
I'm fifty percent heavy metal.
My better half she's modifiable.
How today's women are made.
 Give them five stars for GREAT.

*Author / Jeana Marie Jeffers*

**TAG ME**
**STILETOOS**

*Sing with me.*

I'm a weapon
I'm a ladder
I'm a mallet made of leather.

Woo, Too
Woo, Too
Na, Na, Na

I'm a high top
I'm a stylus
I'm a rocket with a purpose.

Woo, Too
Woo, Too
Na, Na, Na

*Final Verse*
*Do Me Proud!*

I'm a stepper
I'm a cutesy
I'm a flirt within my booties.

Woo, Too
Woo, Too
Na, Na, Na

Woo, Too
Woo, Too
Na, Na, Na

*Author / Jeana Marie Jeffers*

# TAGMEWRITE

**TAG ME**
**STORMS**

It's not much of a parade, when I see you slip and slide.
When they say stay off the streets, you should abide.

The ocean is fierce, especially during this time of year.
So anticipate the thunder, and some major tail spins.

That ice cream cone that you eat from the front yard,
It's a hurricane special, swirling to whip frozen custard.

Though the marvel footage seems to be shot on camera,
I say don't chase the funnel or you might get hammered.

*Author / Jeana Marie Jeffers*

**TAG ME**
**STUBBORN**

I don't want to hear it.
I don't want to hear it.
You know they say that music can soothe the soul.
I don't care!
I don't want to hear it.

I don't want to see it.
I don't want to see it.
You know they say that beauty is in the eyes of the beholder.
I don't care!
I don't want to see it.

I don't want to feel it.
I don't want to feel it.
You know they say love is what makes the world go round.
I don't care!
I don't want to feel it.

I don't want to taste it.
I don't want to taste it.
You know it has been said,
Taste and see that the LORD is good.

## May 3, 2013 — Jeana Marie Jeffers

I don't care!
I don't want to taste it.

I'm not going to do it.
I'm not going to do it.
You know it has been said,
That there is more happiness in giving than there is in receiving.
I don't care!
I'm not going to do it.

Your reluctance to take advantage of using your good senses,
That says much about the kind of person you are.
And so who am I?
I'm not going to tell you.
I'm not going to tell you.

*Author / Jeana Marie Jeffers*

## TAG ME
## SUMO WESTLER

What's my type?
I can answer that question without even thinking about it.

We both have to be on the same EXACT spiritual plane.
That way he's not changing for me, and I'm not for him.
But we see the need for change according to the will,
Of He who brought us together.
So he'll get rid of the ritual salt, and I'll get rid of the crushed pepper.
Because remember, we both now walk in the same name.

Also!
He needs to be big and strong, with extremely tight muscles.
But humble, peaceable, not intimidating,
Or one who loves throwing his weight around.
So he'll have to lose the cloth, and I will have to lose the attitude.
Because remember, we both now walk in the same name.

I'm not picky about his ethnicity,
I'm intoxicated by his body.
And I will choose him over Tarzan to swing in the Jungle with any day.

# TAGMEWRITE

Because remember, we both now walk in the same name.

*Author / Jeana Marie Jeffers*

## TAG ME
## SUNKEN TREASURE

My relationship with you is so much like this.
I search for you and search for you,
Never, ever, does it cross my mind to give up!
Then after finding you, I love you but not right.

It is so hard to express what I feel with words.
Because where you're from they're not written.
So I roll around in all your turquoise and blues.
Spending none, but good to know I'm covered.

After long days being comforted by your luxury,
I return you to the deep knowing where you are.
But don't you worry because I will not stray far.
Afraid that if I do, some pirate will take you away.

*Author / Jeana Marie Jeffers*

## TAG ME
## SYMPHONY ORCHESTRA

Frenchie - Well as our great mentor already explained.
We came on the scene with the money makers.
Obie - No we didn't.
And as usual you have misinterpreted what she said.
When we started entertaining there was no money involved.
Frenchie - No you're wrong.
We held our very first performance in the early 1600's.
And I specifically recall there being some money changers.
Violie – That last statement is correct but only according to that era.
But your first statement is all the way wrong.
Most of us were making melody at the time of the Chronicles.
And at that time as Obie stated, there was no money involved.
We performed out of respect for the King.
Frenchie – Who is telling this story?
Obie – You are! But you're telling it all wrong.

**May 3, 2013** — **Jeana Marie Jeffers**

You need to get your facts straight.
Glockie – Obie I think you need to stop blowing so much hot air,
And let Frenchie finish hanging himself.

Interviewer - Hold on,
Do YOU always dispute with one another like this?
ALL TOGETHER -YES.
Violie - Arguing is the only possible way,
We can give a great performance.
Glockie - So we agreed to disagree.
That way we can get all that negativity out of our systems.
Frenchie - Then the beautiful interviewee sitting right before us,
Obie - Our reason for existing don't leave that out,
Frenchie - Right, we owe our very existence to that TAG.
Therefore when we get on that stage,
We are confident that we are going to do her proud.

*Author / Jeana Marie Jeffers*

**TAG ME**
**TABLE**

I walk around on four legs,
But really I'm elevated.
Then when they broke one,
They said three is better.
Then they changed the design,
And I loved the transformations.
Allow me to give you a demonstration.

GREAT!
Dazzle me.

Ok over there is someone I can help.
I need to help him stack his cold medicine.
And I need to be close by his bedside.
Transform and be green to match his headboard.

NICE.
Transform again.

# TAGMEWRITE

Ok over there is an Architect I bet he could use my help.
I need to be sturdy so that I can help him with his masterpiece.
And I need to tilt, and be equipped with a place to store his tool.
Transform and be green to match the cash inside his wallet.

AWESOME!
Do it one more time.

Ok but since this is the last one I'll make it good.
Ok see that lady over there, she looks like she needs help.
I need to help maintain her status.
So, I need to be an amazing conversation piece.
I want to be round but large enough to seat six.
I want to be completely black, to match the china cabinet.
My four legs should branch off from the balloon middle,
That supports my weight.
Transform and make the wing back chairs lime green,
So as to make all of her friends become green with envy.

Ok I see you like the color green.
But what else can you do?

I can hold books and drinks.
I can hold rooks and kings and queens.
I can hold lamps, candles, and ash trays.
I can hold pool balls and miniature tennis balls.
I can hold chips, and cards, and…..
Well if you name it, I can be it.
And the best part about it,
I just slide to second base and you place your design on first.

WONDERFUL!

*Author / Jeana Marie Jeffers*

**TAG ME**
**TEARS**

I'm a preservative as seasoning is to food.
Sliding down soft mountains till the river is full.

I hide within the cliffs of an emotional estate.

**May 3, 2013** — **Jeana Marie Jeffers**

Then the wind triggers a smear of bitter taste.

I rinse I wash, the island filled with debris.
Dropping crystals in the sockets like detergent.

But when it rains it pours, the words of fame.
Blink and the crocodile will clog up your drain.

*Author / Jeana Marie Jeffers*

## TAG ME
## TELESCOPE

Let me wipe the smudges from my eye.
So I can be your Hubble of the dark sky.
I can see above the deep magnetic hole.
Amazed at how math plays a visible role.

When I lie down, I race back to the top.
And aim my Monocle on the Astronaut.
Walking in boots would be astronomical.
But I'll settle for viewing the phenomenal.

*Author / Jeana Marie Jeffers*

## TAG ME
## TELEVISION

I became an overnight sensation because of my many eyes.
More productive than the English Channel,
Child you better recognize.

I really get turned on whenever I hear my audience clap.
But I'm not too thrilled with your resolution for fine tuning,
I thought the whole idea was pretty whack.

You might think so, but a good choice for a sitter I am not.
Since I can be very addictive in the area of entertainment,
Therefore my suggestion is that you clap again Sherlock.

*Author / Jeana Marie Jeffers*

# TAGMEWRITE

**TAG ME
THE BIBLE**

Sharper than a two edge sword,
Lamp to your foot,
Light to your roadway,
Cannot speak a lie,
Survived the test of time,
And have made the bestsellers list.

**TAG ME
THE CONGA**

Shake your boom boom shake your boom boom,
Come on Serpentine shake your boom boom with me.

You know what? You're impossible.
Everyone else is shuffling to a triple beat,
And you're over here shaking your boom boom.
But this is not the time to shake our booties with this crowd.
If you want to be accepted,
You got to get on the dance floor and step twice but quick,
Then step slower than the other two,
And then kick your way to acceptance.
Just keep right on doing that and we've got it made.

What!
 I did not come here to try and fit in.
That's Ok I did.

Oh! One more thing,
We are not doing any of those crazy moves
From Saturday Night Fever either.

*Author / Jeana Marie Jeffers*

**TAG ME
THE DEAD SEA**

I'm a major attraction for fascinated eyes to see.
They are mostly interested in my Sodom history.

May 3, 2013  **Jeana Marie Jeffers**

Motivated by the tall description of me Biblically,
That is the fire to spark their let me see curiosity.

I'm a hotel chain booked with promise of resurrection.
When the time comes I just cough and VOILA, creation.
As supplier of the embalming fluid for mummification,
They experimented again VOILA, cosmetic foundation.

My number one ingredient can be hazardous to all fish.
The belief that it's impossible to drown in me is a myth.
So go with your instinct and forfeit the crazy death wish.
Thank you for your time, now listen to Beethoven's 5th.

*Author / Jeana Marie Jeffers*

**TAG ME**
**THE FOUR WINDS**

Let me blow on your hair like King Kong.
Caress your face until the height of dawn.
Our love comes at you from all directions.
A truce is called for the day of inspection.

Not everything we toss at you is vanity.
Instability enables us to keep our sanity.
Although we want very much to commit,
But we would be tempestuous hypocrites.

And if not for the four Angels persistence,
This breezy affair would fly in the distance.
So we're working on staying nice and calm.
And respect the wishes of God's Kingdom.

*Author / Jeana Marie Jeffers*

**TAG ME**
**THE HUMAN BODY**

I'm wonderfully made even if I'm not all there.
Some have less and others have new repairs.
But it seems to be those with, living in despair.

# TAGMEWRITE

Calling those without handicapped, that's unfair.

Especially since their coping mechanism is norm.
With help they appreciate being able to move on.
And to those caring for me from the day I was born,
You'll reap rewards for not treating me like a thorn.

*Author / Jeana Marie Jeffers*

**TAG ME**
**THE MARRIAGE OF A WASHER AND DRYER**

Scoot over!
You're invading my space.

Well excuse me your highness,
This load has me feeling a little bloated,
And that is why I rocked in your space.
I was only trying to balance.

Bloated, Balance,
Those are two words I never want to hear.
They could only mean one thing,
That I'm going to work that much harder,
To sweat out all that excess water.

That's right!
Just ignore the fact that I'm over worked too.
I'm getting a little tired of all our conversations,
Spinning off in one direction,
And then they recycle and end up being about you.

That is just not true.
I care ….
Hey!
You know what!
Something crazy just popped up.
Instead of us working side by side,
They should have put me on top.

Why?
Do you think that all of your complaining

## May 3, 2013 — Jeana Marie Jeffers

Would go over better if you were on top of me?
Well think again partner!
I don't want all your nasty sweat rolling down my back.

No.
I was actually thinking along the lines of my weight
Helping you stay in your place.

Man.
You had better shut your trap immediately,
Or you're going to regret it when I throw something
Dirty up in it.

What did I do now?
That is just like a woman,
Always taking what you say out of context.

*Author / Jeana Marie Jeffers*

**TAG ME**
**THE MOON**

At the peak of dawn I can still see you,
Winking at the Owl going Who, Who,
All the while the time table is spinning,
In comes the cycle with a new beginning.

I beckon for your attention when half full,
Though justice is eclipsed by divine rule,
Laughing at the sparks tickling my insides,
Joyful as we pass to give another high five.

I bring out the best in lovers everywhere,
Listening to Michael sing Got to Be There,
Yet some do whisper look up at the lunatic,
They still love seeing this faithful night flick.

*Author / Jeana Marie Jeffers*

# TAGMEWRITE

**TAG ME
THE OCEAN**

I hear you calling me from the Buoyancy Vaughn View,
The words are come pass time current passes through.
Accepting your invitation like an Angel I hover above,
Then I photo shoot your blue body that fits like a glove.

I wish my heart were like yours so I too could sustain life,
Just seeing you in motion can help anyone sleep at night.
As I sleep dreaming about your adaptable circumstances,
I discover the sunken secret how you dissolve substances.

So the very next day I gear up to dive into your deep fold,
After about a minute of contact the body ceases to be cold.
I then dive for the bottom with plankton brushing my sides,
Then you place in my hand treatment and then say goodbye.

As I return above your surface I breast stroke the final mile,
Clutching the remedy that you gave and doing so with a smile.
I thank you for the lesson in love and will guard it forever,
Until we meet again my friend you are a wonderful treasure.

*Author / Jeana Marie Jeffers*

**TAG ME
THE RIVER**

I know dear,

I'm filled with your favorite creation embodied with 50-70 percent.
I'm writing because my mouth is streaming with resourceful events.

To get things flowing, in May, they have planned several casino trips.
I'm looking forward to just cruising along with the weight of the ship.

The middle of June, lumberjacks have scheduled a logrolling contest.
Weeks of preparation, for some vandals left beer bottles in my chest.

And lastly in July, we're going to recreate the adventures of Huck Finn.
Naturally they'll symbolize me as the mode of escape for him and Jim.

**May 3, 2013**    **Jeana Marie Jeffers**

I'm so excited, and can't wait to see you.
But for now I'll hold on to the memories
Of hearing your stories while bathing you.

Au Revoir!

*Author / Jeana Marie Jeffers*

## TAG ME
## THE SUN

Well my story is probably not as touching as hers.
But I would follow her for life wherever she goes.

Though we do have something we share in common.
Her brother and my sister, share the same time space.

Though this is how we differ, sister did not get first choice.
I trusted our maker knew who would be the perfect match.

And that He did, He placed us exactly where we belong.
So I feared for nothing, forgetting that this is His song.

I'm truly happy that it was Day and I to be united.
Sister winks every new horizon and says to us, Great Job!

Oh how I do love it, when my energy lights up Days smile.
And watching her skip through the seasons set to my dial.

But this is not about a love story between me and the Day.
It is about making sure that each of us rises their own way.

*Author / Jeana Marie Jeffers*

## TAG ME
## THUMBELINA

My heart is blue from the lost of you,
Flying in my lonely space;
Until over the cuckoo's nest I flew.

# TAGMEWRITE

But I'm trying my best to emotionally heal,
By sharing with others how rejection can make one feel,
Therefore I sung about those memories in baritone fairytale.

From the very moment you entered this world,
Not once did you consider giving our love a whirl,
Yet I treasured your worth like a precious pearl.

And when you escaped with your life from the family of knots,
I waited for your return, as my heart for you went flip flop,
But you drifted far away to be captured by the claws of Camelot.

Then once again I saw the possibility of us bonding,
For the friends of Camelot snubbed you with stern reprimanding.
Although that form of rejection did not affect your fine standing.

For me though your trials pushed you even farther from my life,
You ended up falling in love with a prince that made you his wife.
Then you grew wings and changed your name to Umm.

Who Are You?
And that is how rejection makes one feel,
It hurts you to the point of where you just want to forget the real.

*Author / Jeana Marie Jeffers*

**TAG ME**
**TIME MACHINE**

Slipping in and out of life with nowhere to go and nowhere to be,
I decide to take a few trips and see what challenges awaits me.
So the first place I listed was a visit to Egypt.

So there I was surrounded by kilns of limestone,
Ready to assist my Brothers and Sisters erect the Great Sphinx.
After about one week of hard labor I decided my work was done.
It was now time for me to move on.
But making my departure wasn't easy.
Those Egyptians weren't too fond of the word freedom.
In fact they were advocates of slave labor.
So like Moses I high tailed it up out of there.

**May 3, 2013**     **Jeana Marie Jeffers**

But I did not have to part the red sea.
I allowed modern technology to set me free.

The second place on my list to visit was Rome.
I must have had my timing off,
Because I was going there to help erect the Coliseum,
But I ended up in the arena as a Gladiator ready for combat.
So quickly I pushed the button on my metal vest.
But if I had been one second off then it would have been curtains.

I then set my sights on China.
Great just in time they have probably a mile or two left to go.
So the next eight hours we work shoulder to shoulder.
Then we look back and say, mission accomplished. 任务完成
They said it in their language and I just nodded.
Then they said, 吃的时候
I wasn't sure what that meant
But after being lead to the dinner table,
I knew they must have said.
Time to eat!
But after taking one look at the spread,
It did not look anything like what they serve in the U.S
So as not be disrespectful or insulting,
I pushed the button.

There are many more places that I would like to visit and lend a hand.
But right now I really would like to just go forward.
And since I have no idea what the future holds.
I'm just going to return me and my wonderful invention to the present.

*Author / Jeana Marie Jeffers*

**TAG ME**
**TUNNEL**

Quick!
Duck in here.
Hit the lights!
Earrrrrrrrrrrrrrongah
Earrrrrrrrrrrrrrrrrrrrongah
Zooooooooooooooooooom

# TAGMEWRITE

URRRRRRRRRRRRR
BOOM!
Maybe we would have been safer,
If you had listened to me,
And we had fled, by way of tracks.
It's your fault.
If you hadn't said hit the lights,
That would not have happened.
You didn't get hit did you?
NO!
Well let's keep it moving.
There is bound to be some more light, at the end.

*Author / Jeana Marie Jeffers*

**TAG ME**
**TYRANNOSAURUS REX**

Thump, Thump
Thumpa Thump.
Thump Thump Thump Thump
Thumpa Thump.
Thump, Thump
Thumpa Thump.
Thump Thump Thump Thump
Thumpa Thump.
HEY!

That's the music I bring to the BYOF party.
But I wonder why the hostess changed the party status to BYOF?
I guess some invited guess has a serious problem with self control.
Well no problem, I think I have enough on this platter to go around.

Chomp.
Ooh that taste good.
Chomp.
Umm I like that too.
Let me try something on the other side of the tray.
Chomp.
Ooh Yummy!
Chomp, Chomp, Chomp, Chomp.
Oh shucks!

**May 3, 2013** — **Jeana Marie Jeffers**

It's all gone.
Now what am I gonna do?
Maybe someone else brought plenty,
And they won't even notice that I didn't bring any.
Besides they all jump when they hear my music,
So I think everythang is gonna be alright.

Thump, Thump
Thumpa Thump.
Thump Thump Thump Thump
Thumpa Thump.
Thump, Thump
Thumpa Thump.
Thump Thump Thump Thump
Thumpa Thump.
Hey!

Oh Lord there he is and look, once again he showed up empty handed.
What we gon do Lizzie?
Hide!

*Author / Jeana Marie Jeffers*

**TAG ME**
**VITAMINS**

FRED – Ok everybody let's play this game,
And describe this tag with letters A-Z.
If you miss, or your description don't make sense,
You're OUT.
The last person to stay alive wins.
So, I'm going to start us off.

FRED
A - Absorption
WILMA
B -
BARNEY
C -
BETTY
D – Dino

# TAGMEWRITE

BARNEY
Betty honey how in the world did you come up with Dino?

BETTY
Well he is one of us isn't he?

FRED
Ok, I'll let that pass this time Betty.

BETTY
Thanks Fred.

FRED
Ok whose turn is it?
Oh it's on me right.
E - Essential

WILMA
F – Flintstones

FRED
Ok!
Wilma both you and Betty are making the clues to obvious.
One more response like that and you're both out of the game.

WILMA
Oh Fred.
You're taking all the fun out of the game.
I thought you would be proud of me for using our last name.

FRED
Uh Huh!
Moving right along,
Barney my main man it's your turn.

BARNEY
With all these unnecessary interruptions coming from you Fred,
I forget what letter we're on.

FRED
G! G!

BARNEY
Laughing,
A key, key, key!
Ok don't pop a blood vessel.
G – Generic

FRED
Good one Barn.

BETTY
H – Hormones

FRED
That's awesome Betty.
I – Iron

WILMA
Umm let me see.
J – Jujube
And don't you start criticizing my answer Fred.
Do your research I did not make that name up.

FRED
Grumbles, this is just like when we play scrabble,
She always has to show off.

BARNEY
Laughing,
A Key, key, key!
K – I don't dare say Phylloquinone or Fred will have a fit.
Kefir

BETTY
L – Lecithin

FRED
Umm
M –
Umm

# TAGMEWRITE

WILMA
What the matter dear are the responses getting too complicated?

FRED
No! I just need to think.

Jeopardy theme plays in the background.
M – Mr. Slate.

WILMA AND BETTY OBJECTING
No, No, No,

BETTY
You didn't like it when Wilma said Flintstones
Or when I responded with Dino,
You even threatened to oust us out of the game.
So your use of Mr. Slate should not count either.

WILMA
I agree with Betty Fred.

FRED
Ladies, ladies, ladies,
Come on let's be fair.
Didn't I give you another chance?

BARNEY
OK Fred,
We give you another chance to give another clue.
But if you mess up this time, you're OUT!
Laughing,
 A key, key key!

FRED
Ok,
M – Magnesium

BARNEY
Nice come back.

WILMA
N – Niacin

**May 3, 2013** — Jeana Marie Jeffers

BARNEY
O – Omega 6

BETTY
P – Peppermint

WILMA
Nice one Betty.
I just love the power of peppermint.
It helps my digestive system.
Helps to get rid of my heart burn,
Brought on by you know who.

FRED
Alright that is enough yickety, yacking.
Let's get on with the game.

WILMA
OK,
It's on you.

FRED
R – Riboflavin
Now deal with that!

WILMA
S – Sage

FRED
I'm not even going to question that,
With a response like that,
It is obvious that it is getting close to dinner time.

WILMA
WHAT EVER…………..

BARNEY
T – Thiamine

BETTY

# TAGMEWRITE

U – Uncle Tex

FRED
Betty no matter how much I appreciate that response,
YOU'RE OUT!

BETTY
Ha, Ha, Ha
I don't care,
I just could not leave Uncle Tex out.

FRED
V- Valerian

WILMA
Fred you're cheating,
There is no way I'm convinced that,
You came up with that response all by yourself.
Gazoo where are you?

FRED
Wilma honey it's just a game.
And I'm insulted that you would even think,
That I would stoop to something so lame.

WILMA
Grumbling,
Ooh I could just spit.
 W – Hanna & Barbera
Oh!
Now see what you made me do.

FRED
I'm sorry honey,
But you lose.

BARNEY
Laughing,
A key, Key, Key
X - Xylitol

FRED

May 3, 2013    **Jeana Marie Jeffers**

Umm
I was certain that,
Barn would not come up with anything.
Y -
Hold on,
I know it.
Piss, Gazoo, Gazoo.
I need you buddy.
Come to my rescue.

BARNEY
I'm waiting Fred.

FRED
I got nothing.

BARNEY
I win!
Yahoo, game over!
No, in the words of my best friend,
Yabba
Dabba
Do!

And the final two responses are,
Y – Yucca and Z – Zink

*Author / Jeana Marie Jeffers*

**TAG ME**
**VOLCANO**

Oh my goodness as Shirley Temple would say,
Too many spicy foods have upset my tummy.
I feel so bloated that I could just let it all go,
But all this gas could do some serious damage.

Whew!
Things are starting to really heat up in here,
I might have to take the entire bottle of Tums.
Burp.

# TAGMEWRITE

Wow that feels a little better.
Burp.
Oh, oh I hope I did not get any on you,
Because that little bit just might burn.
Burp.
I think my tummy is starting to settle,
And hopefully the next time my insides won't explode.

*Author / Jeana Marie Jeffers*

**TAG ME
ZEBRA**

Doppler - I try hard to keep things civilized around here.
But you bronco's just insist on being divided.
You run in packs,
Trying to see which one of you can outrun the other.
You fight one another and you're of the same color.
And they say we're wild, and hard to tame.

Now let's go over this one more time.
Repeat after Me!
I Dark Moon, Little Moon, Silver Moon, Grey Moon,
Brown Derby Splash and Herbie,
Dark Moon - Herbie! Naw not Herbie.
Yes Herbie.
Dark Moon - But he's just an Ass.
Herbie - Excuse Me!
I'm part Ass and part Horse that makes me a Mule.
Get a clue!
Doppler - You see, Herbie is part of the Herd family.
So are you going to say it or not?
(RELUCTANT)
Ok.
I Dark Moon, Little Moon, Silver Moon, Grey Moon,
Brown Derby, Splash and I Herbie,
Promise to do better and be more like Doppler.
(GRUMBLING)
Promise to do better and be more like Doppler.
Because if we don't.
Because if we don't.
All the other paints are going to be done away with.

And there won't be anything left but black and white.
All the other paints are going to be done away with.
And there won't be anything left but black and white.
Thank You!
Now go somewhere and do some grazing.

(TROTTING AWAY WITH HERBIE BRINGING UP THE REAR)
Splash - Ok, although I'm safe.
Refresh my memory.
How did Doppler become leader of the pack?

Grey Moon - He's the fastest runner out of the pack.
He must have got in lots of exercise in his country.
And he studied magic there.
He said that is how he earned his stripes.
So do you want all of us to end up looking like him?

Splash - NO! I like my paint.

Doppler - Then be very, very careful not to start a stampede,
Or try to buck the order of things.

Splash – Where did he come from?
Herbie – He's also very sneaky.
Dark Moon – Well he can stay up front.
You can't miss him, he's a bull's-eye.
(EVERYONE LAUGHING)

*Author / Jeana Marie Jeffers*

# TAGMEWRITE

## ABOUT THE AUTHOR

Who Am I?

I'm a dreamer though I don't always believe that they are real.
Growing as a woman, I lived at best with only pessimistic ideals.
Now because of life changes, my hormones do constantly insist.
That I no longer go through life as an unbeliever, but an optimist.

So, I react favorably to the prodding and write my many words.
Realizing I share something in common with all YOU fellow birds.
I'm a living example and encourage YOU, to spread YOUR wings.
Believe. Let not FEAR stifle your airway, to breathe good things.

With all the ink of my heart, I paint YOUR eyes with amazing talent.
Enjoy all that YOU read, and try to absorb it all with perfect balance.
NOW! No question about it. YOU know, I know, exactly Who I Am.
I'm the woman with many dreams and will write them for my FAM.

Thank YOU!
*Author / Jeana Marie Jeffers*

www.ingramcontent.com/pod-product-compliance
Lightning Source LLC
Chambersburg PA
CBHW041619220426
43661CB00046B/1502